Lisa is a good friend of mine, and she ha[...]
When you turn the last page, not only will you know her better, you'll
understand yourself more fully. This book is full to the brim with
truth and authenticity, love and compassion. By_____

—**Bob Goff**, author, *New York Times* bestselling *Love Does*

This book is about a spiritual journey, and I've had the privilege of
walking alongside my friend Lisa through many of these passages in
the fifteen years of our friendship. Lisa is one of the most truly creative people I know, and one of the most soulful. Her writing style is
as beautiful as her songs are, and her journey will feel familiar to so
many—joy and pain, disillusionment and discovery. She's a brave and
brilliant person, and I'm so thankful for this book.

—**Shauna Niequist**, author, *Present over Perfect* and *Bread and Wine*

Lisa Gungor's beautifully written memoir is transparent, raw, and
honest. She welcomes us into the hardest moments of her life with
compassion and empathy, taking us on a journey of self-discovery
that at times surprises and at other times has us screaming out, "Me
too!" Her story is about the beauty and strength that are born in and
through pain, uncertainty, and fear. I finished this book eager to find
the gorgeous truth that each moment in my life has to teach me.

—**Sarah Drew**, American actress, producer, and director

The Most Beautiful Thing I've Seen is intimate in a way few books
are, so bring along a box of tissues to blot the tears for the journey. It's
worth it: this work will show you the miracles all around you, especially in the dark places.

—**Mike McHargue**, cofounder, The Liturgists;
author, *Finding God in the Waves*

In her book, Lisa gives us the most precious gift of all—herself. We
read the story of mother and daughter, and the transformation of that
daughter into a mother herself—one unbroken line of womanhood, a

journey of becoming and letting go all at the same time. This book is honest and breathtakingly beautiful. It is as much a woman's story as it is an invitation into the greater story, a story of opening, oneness, and the painfully awe-inspiring journey of being human.

—Hillary McBride, author, *Mothers, Daughters, and Body Image*

If there's anyone in the world you want to teach you about wonder, it's Lisa. When you read this book, your eyes will be opened to the beauty that's already around you, to all the ways the very life you're living right now is calling you to be in awe. It will take you deeper, and make you laugh and cry and feel at home in your own skin. This book is a gift.

—Allison Fallon, author, *Indestructible*; founder, Becoming Indestructible

With the skill of a wordsmith and the heart of a poet, Lisa invites the reader into an experience of humanity, family, and faith that breaks the heart and knits it back together with a greater degree of strength, courage, vulnerability, and love than it had before the breaking.

—Caterina Scorsone, star in *Grey's Anatomy* and *Private Practice*

Lisa's heart beats so vividly and passionately throughout every page of this book. What an incredible gift it is to be welcomed into her memories and experiences; it is sacred space. And what a privilege to learn from and be inspired by such brave vulnerability. As each of us stumbles into our own mysteries of faith, love, and family, Lisa's words help us to stumble more gracefully.

—Ryan O'Neal, Sleeping At Last

I will never forget the first time Lisa and I met. She instantly felt like family. She is genuine and warm, and to know her is to adore her, and to be known and adored in return. These qualities saturate everything she puts her hands to. Her words, whether spoken in conversation, sung in song, or written in this book, create a wild sense of wonder and meaning which is often lacking in our day to day. I am so thankful she has chosen to share these words with the world.

—**Heather Avis**, author, speaker, advocate

This is a delightful memoir, masterfully depicting a woman's reckoning with her evolving faith and the contentious voices of family, tribe, and religion. Its heartfelt hilarity and antidotal wisdom are soul stirring while thoroughly convicting. Lisa's vision of beauty summons us back to the truth about ourselves, gently nudging us toward wholeness and love. I highly endorse Lisa and this book.

—**William Matthews**, Artist x Advocate; songwriter

This thing drips with lived wisdom that only a wordsmith like Lisa could give us.

—**Jason Petty**, Propaganda artist; cohost,
The Red Couch Podcast

What can I say? This book reveals the spacious soul, tender heart, and frightfully creative mind of the most incredible woman I've ever met. In these artfully crafted words and heartwrenching stories, you'll not only be inspired to see the world anew but also see why this woman has stolen my heart so completely.

—**Michael Gungor**, musician; composer; author,
The Crowd, the Critic, and the Muse;
cofounder, The Liturgists

THE MOST BEAUTIFUL THING I'VE SEEN

THE MOST BEAUTIFUL THING I'VE SEEN

OPENING YOUR EYES TO WONDER

LISA GUNGOR

ZONDERVAN

The Most Beautiful Thing I've Seen
Copyright © 2018 by Lisa Gungor

Requests for information should be addressed to:
Zondervan, *3900 Sparks Dr. SE, Grand Rapids, Michigan 49546*

ISBN 978-0-310-35043-9 (softcover)

ISBN 978-0-310-35046-0 (audio)

ISBN 978-0-310-35044-6 (ebook)

Any Internet addresses (websites, blogs, etc.) and telephone numbers in this book are offered as a resource. They are not intended in any way to be or imply an endorsement by Zondervan, nor does Zondervan vouch for the content of these sites and numbers for the life of this book.

Author is represented by The Christopher Ferebee Agency, www.christopherferebee.com.

Art direction: Curt Diepenhorst
Interior design: Denise Froehlich

First printing April 2018 / Printed in the United States of America

For Amelie and Lucie,
my two gurus

CONTENTS

PROLOGUE

Dear Mother,

It is no secret, we don't see eye to eye. But this wasn't always the case. You saw me at my birth, held me close to your chest, saw me more clearly than anyone else. We looked out the same windows, woke to the same sounds and house. We walked the same terra-cotta tile to the kitchen each morning. As a child I would run up to your legs and hug them hard. I'd look up at you and ask questions about this world we shared. You gave your best answers, bought cartoon bandaids for my skinned knees, said prayers for my soul. You gave me what you had as a mother and a teacher, in physicality and philosophy. You were the bedtime storyteller, midnight monster-chaser. My comfort and springboard. That's how it goes, isn't it? Parents hand over what they know to the child, and down the line it is handed.

But what I have learned is that each life takes it own shape. You can't control its future or confine it to its beginning, because a springboard is just that—a jumping off point. You had your own beginning, your own hallways to wander and concrete to run down. I often think our decisions and beliefs are simply a matter of personal choice, but it's never as simple as that. Our assumptions and conclusions are always related to circumstance.

Your parents handed down rules, beliefs, and a lens through which you could view the world. Your experiences caused you to accept, reject, or adjust those perspectives and assumptions.

And so it is that neither my child home nor yours is the beginning of our stories. No.

Our stories point to family trees, politics, and religions (the good and the bad or the lack thereof). The circumstances that influence our lives are vast and interconnected with everything and everyone in ways none of us will ever be able to map. I can't draw lines between dots on paper in order to understand just how I got to this city, this porch, or just how you and I took such different paths.

When I was a child, I knew I could tell you anything, and I did on most counts. You were Super Woman and my very best friend—a rare find. I never would have imagined that you and I would someday face such a conflict. Though conflict is common between parents and children, it doesn't hurt any less. I came from your body, walk around on this earth with hands and a laugh and a heart like yours. We used to sound so similar cheering for the same home team and president, but now, now there is this difference. Now we don't understand the other and I know I haven't really explained why.

After I left home, there were the phone calls and visits, but I stopped letting you in on the deep inner shifts and turns.

I hid it from you because for so long you had been my guide, the teacher showing me how to tie my shoes, how to write my name in cursive, and how to love. I didn't let you see the full extent of these shifts because I felt guilty and most of all afraid.

I was afraid of telling you the full truth, especially when it came to faith. It is difficult for any parent to let go of their child's hand; I know how that feels now. Mother fear is a monster.

So I sifted words. I spoke cautiously or not at all. So you, along with everyone else, found out important things about my life through headlines and secondhand conversations. I am so sorry for that. You couldn't see the shift, so you too were afraid.

You couldn't see me on my knees begging God to show me if I was wrong. You also didn't see just why I fell in love with the one I did; didn't know how it felt when he and I hunkered together laughing in the pouring rain. How his eyes looked into mine and undid me.

You didn't see our best times or our worst and how that molded us through the years, didn't witness how ridiculous and wild our dance parties were and are—me all flailing knees and elbows and he all Puerto Rican spice. I knew he was a keeper. You didn't see the faces I saw, the stories I heard, the secrets I discovered, didn't see me drowning in a belief that used to be my lifeboat. I had to jump ship. And you didn't see what I saw afterward.

Now we don't understand each other.

So this book is my attempt to finally talk about it. I will do my best to tell you and anyone else who will listen about the magic that I have learned to see and the really painful things I had to experience to help me see it.

This story is about perspective—where I started, what broke and died and opened up, and the incomprehensible beauty I see all around and within me now. The poet Rumi wrote, "the wound is where the light enters you." I've found this to be true in ways I never would have imagined.

Perspective

My first drawing class in college began simply enough. The teacher walked to the easel and put a dot on the paper.

"What is this?" she asked.

Someone said, "A dot."

Another student, "A point . . . er, I guess that's the same?"

"Hmm," the teacher said while nodding her head. She kept looking at us while slowly pacing.

"A ball," a girl said.

"A line," I said.

The teacher looked at me and raised her eyebrows.

"A cylinder," said another student. And the teacher began to smile as a new set of answers ensued imagining the thing we saw on the board from a different perspective.

"Nail."

"Pencil."

"Tower."

"A line, which is really the side of a rectangle, which is a door, which is . . ."

It may be a dot, but maybe it's also something else. It's all perspective, isn't it?

I see this; you see that. Two people can look at the same

thing but not see the same thing. One person can look at the color blue and see a deep cobalt hue, another a light sea-foam green. One person can look at a piece of art and see a striking landscape; another sees only blotches and turns on their heel, unimpressed. One person looks out at the ocean and sees thrill and joy while the other sees sharks and drowning.

One looks at a cross and sees redemption and peace—the cross saved them. Another sees this same cross and it embodies violence; it was around the neck of the man who took their innocence in a dark room. One person can look at America and see freedom, the soil where dreams come true—"land of the free, home of the brave!" But maybe a survivor of Hiroshima sees only corruption—this is the country that set their family on fire.

We see things differently because our histories or circumstances give us differing viewpoints. One can look at a child with almond-shaped eyes, small nose, different speech, and see only a syndrome; maybe they see an opportunity for a miracle to happen. Another sees the child as a miracle that already has happened.

Reality is one thing to you and another to me, but none of us sees it for what it is. My brain is putting information together without my knowing; it's filling in gaps, taking that bit of light into my retina, sending signals to my brain, triggering memories and recalling the color I know to be blue. But some people don't see blue at all.

Sight—it has come in moments.

In sunsets that screamed with color and love that left me unable to speak a word. What a rare and hard thing when something gives us eyes to see what we previously couldn't. Sometimes my heart sees, and sometimes it just doesn't.

It's all clear, then my eyes cloud over and I feel the pull of my previous perspective—out of habit, out of comfort or maybe pure laziness. Or maybe it comes from the idea that I just really need to try harder, be better, smarter, more talented, and God, I really need to be fixed. I did it better as a child, this whole "seeing with your heart" business. So it makes sense that my search for new perspective, for new eyes and a heart to see, would be splintered and cracked open by a child.

The journey toward new sight can be equal parts beautiful and all out hell. But it comes to all of us the same—slowly, in moments separating old from new, before from after. Moments that split time or split our very souls, and we suddenly see life as we have never seen it before.

PART 1

DOT

Imagine you are born on a dot. Your dot is your home. Your dot is where your caretaker cradles you, where you first go to school. You learn about math and how there are mean kids and nice kids and just where you fit or don't. It's where you adventure for hours, discovering the magic in the soil and the trees and how your body shifts, moves, feels in it all. Your dot is the tribe you were born into, your vantage point in the world. You learn a lot while living on this dot.

Where the Light Comes In (Part 1)

I hung the pictures my mother made me above the crib. She stitched them for my sister and me when we were little, and now they would be in a room with my own two daughters—needlepoint girls with a puppy and a cat in aged yellow frames. I straightened them, stepped back, and examined whether they were crooked.

As I situated the space for a second pair of little feet to romp around in, scenes flashed by—I imagined her tiny face and felt her skin, saw myself looking into her eyes, breathing her in.

I saw Michael and me sending newborn photos to family and friends, laughing at how she looked like a small wrinkly old man, as they always do. I saw our older daughter, Amelie, meeting her for the first time; how excited she would be to have her very own real-life sister to dress up and boss around. I saw us singing all the absurd and sappy songs we make up at night because making up ridiculous songs is kind of our thing.

I saw Amelie holding her sister's tiny chubby hands as she wobbled about, learning to walk. They would run into their room together, screaming like mad as I chased them, telling secrets under covers while I told them to go to sleep for the hundredth time. I saw them calling each other when one felt heartbreak or had a first kiss, and yelling at each other for stealing clothes, stinking up the bathroom, not having enough privacy, for the slew of other things that come with having a sibling.

I realized I had plans for these two little lives already, yet I was only situating yellow frames on a wall.

In weeks the pregnancy became complicated. I was put on bedrest, saw my trusty OBGYN every two weeks plus a specialist every week. The specialist informed us my placenta, which I named Janice, was crapping out on me. Ol' Janice, she was a swell ol' gal but just didn't want to go the distance. "It's common with smokers," said the specialist, though I didn't smoke. Rather, I drank spinach, kale, and magical human-building smoothies with vitamin powder. But Ol' Janice the Placenta didn't care. She rejected it all.

"She's just small," the specialist said.

I looked to Michael for some sort of second opinion. "She's just small; she's our little squish. She's going to be fine." Michael's hug made me feel safe, but I could see he wasn't certain he believed himself.

We went about our week, had another checkup. We were about to head out of the specialist's office when he calmly told us that not enough blood was flowing to her brain. "Don't be alarmed, but things have changed and we need her to come out today."

Michael called family and texted friends, "She's coming soon!" And though the doctor said not to be worried, we both knew "not enough blood to the brain" was more than slightly concerning.

We anxiously walked into the hospital, onto the labor and delivery floor, and there stood our friends Bre and Jamie with a dozen donuts. Jamie is a lumberjackish hipster with a heart of gold. Bre is fiery and warm and can heal anything with her cooking. My mother went to get me some water and blankets as we settled into our room. My person-for-life, Rachael, came in, hugged us all, ate a donut, then found her spot in the delivery room as my doctor put her hand in uncomfortable places.

My mother rushed in with ice, out with news to the waiting room as I paced the delivery room. Contractions came closer and closer while Michael swayed in rhythm with me.

One moment I was eating a grape popsicle, another bearing down with the focus of a woman warrior queen. Our baby girl's heart rate fell drastically. I pushed hard. It was quick, and in a single minute, our world changed.

It feels like only moments ago she came from my body and lay on my chest. Her five-pound frame slight, fragile. Her skin on my skin. I kissed her head, and once again, as with my first, I felt the surreal emotions that come with holding your child. This was her, the one I almost miscarried, the one kicking my ribs so hard, letting me know she would be strong, the one Amelie would sing to at night and say, "Sister! Don't be a stinky butt! I love you so much!" Here she was, finally safe.

I held her close and with awe as happy tears came. Michael leaned in, kissed me, touched her head. Matthew Perryman Jones' "Land of the Living" played in the background. But she wasn't moving much. She felt limp and motionless, not at all like my first baby felt. I pulled her in, wondering why she didn't make a sound. I watched as her skin turned blue.

A nurse swiftly took her, saying something about waking her

up a bit. Our tiny girl lay like a rag in her hands. No cries, no movement. Nurses huddled and whispered, moved fast and sent secret glances. Michael and I held hands, confused by the rising tension. Then finally a single little cry, and I exhaled, smiled. A nurse walked around to the right side of my bed. She turned, faced me directly, tucked a strand of hair behind her ear. She wrung her hands a bit, eyes shifting, looking at mine, then darting to the floor. It felt like she needed to tell me something, so I nodded, encouraged her with a slight smile to go ahead. Her voice shook as she began, "Your baby has signs consistent with Down syndrome. She has a line in her hand, and her eyes . . ." and that's all I heard. I saw her mouth moving but heard nothing.

It is right here. A two-word definition gives me a limited viewpoint for my child. My brain is filling in gaps, drawing on memories, telling me what to feel and just how to see things.

My heart pounded as the key scraped metal and my hand faltered. I cursed, then tried again. Hands shaking as the key slid into place. It turned and I opened the car door in a craze. This was the escape. Because something was running fast after me. A feeling, a panic, an animal sprang out of ground that used to be solid and secure.

Maybe I could outrun it. Maybe if I held my breath long enough, reality would be placated, the ground would resolidify. Maybe if I ran, the animal would tire and retreat. I reversed, then plowed forward out of the parking garage, out onto the city street, turning.

My mind played a scene of two walking along a cracked sidewalk in dim light whispering words that scared me to the core. Is the story I have believed my whole life a sham? Is the entirety of my belief constructed of circumstance and ancestry and nothing more?

I saw my child-self in our back yard, feet hitting the black mat of a trampoline and water spraying high. I landed on my back and looked up at the blue above, wondering just what life would hold for my older self. I never imagined it like this. I drove on, then saw myself in the hospital, saw our baby turn blue, saw our career crash, and saw myself as a terribly weak failure who couldn't pull herself together.

These moments folded and bent the reality I knew to be true into an object. A thing to be walked around, viewed from different sides and angles until I saw it as something else, until I saw through it. I knew it was me in all of those scenes, but somehow it felt like someone else. It didn't feel like me on that trampoline as a child jumping high. Just how did I get from there to this?

I turned onto Interstate 25, drove fast for the mountains. I attempted to outrun the scenes my mind kept replaying, outrun the feeling that I couldn't do this, that I wasn't strong enough. Outrun the animal. The animal—was it the darkest part of myself? Finally aware of itself, raising its head to bite? It's a terrifying thing to see this dark side, the side that feels helpless and enraged. Like a domesticated animal poked and prodded until it turns wild and violent, desperate to free itself. It used to be a kind, helpful companion, but there were too many tricks. I drove on white-knuckled and all was silent until I found myself staring toward the mountains and screaming at the top of my lungs like a wide-eyed crazed thing. A stranger driving in the car next to me stared at me, open-mouthed and slightly terrified.

The first few moments that our baby experienced her first

breaths, first sights, first time being held in my arms, she was purely perfect. Then in minutes she was given a definition. We were given a lens for viewing her with, and my perspective shifted right at her very start. The definition "Down syndrome" is packed full of emotions, full of ideas that are only ideas, and I was diving headfirst into all of the darkest ones that screamed, "She won't make it, and you won't either."

I know the feeling; we all know it. We want to thrive, live brilliant lives, and experience love that never disappoints or leaves us. We want our differences celebrated, not pushed to the sidelines or discarded. We want to live the human experience with our eyes and hearts open, but it's often so hurtful we can't help but close up.

It is the drive in every relationship—will you really see me and love me? But to really see someone, your perspective will bend and shift at some point. To be able to see, we first must realize that all of our constructs are illusions.

He is a person, but he is more than a person. She is a baby with a condition, but she is not a condition. We are looking through a cloudy lens, trying to see, walking around half blind, half asleep, until something is unlatched. Or born.

Something calls to us, tells us there is more than what we see, more than what we know. It whispers, "Hey, look this way. I have something you have never seen before."

Trampoline

Reality is only a Rorschach ink-blot, you know.

—ALAN WATTS

I was six when the water splashed high, suspended, then fell with the sun dancing in each drop. My feet hit the black, stretched mat, sending a hundred watery prisms glittering up around my legs. Drops slid off my skin, some drying up fast from the hot sun while others filtered through the tight weave, from top to underneath, gathered themselves in a huddle, then dropped like gymnasts to the grass below. I bore my weight down and jumped harder, propelled myself higher this time, stretched out my arms and became a bird. My body laid out flat in midair and I fell back onto the trampoline, bounced until the mat shivered while I gazed with blue eyes into a blue sky.

I felt curious and adventuresome, the world alive with every crack and hum. Magic called in every tree, rock, slimy thing, and cloud. I looked up. In the sky resided a dog, a clown, a ray of sunshine breaking through a parting in the clouds, and

I thought maybe this was it: Jesus was finally coming back this very moment. I should have worn something more appropriate. A swimsuit showed too much leg, really all the leg, and I wasn't sure what Jesus thought about that. But his dad was God, and God made the leg, so I assumed he'd be cool with it, considering it was the second coming and all. And didn't everyone lose all of their clothes anyway when they were "taken up"? If I left the swimsuit behind anyway, revealing all my private parts to the neighbors plus Jesus and God, the swimsuit must be an okay thing to wear for the time being.

The ray of sunlight faded as the clouds merged back together. I guessed today wasn't the day.

I looked into the blue sky and blinked away drops of water. I imagined sitting up on that dog cloud and looking back at myself. My body was a tiny dot. Then I imagined I flew farther out until I couldn't see my body but only my little town. It too was a tiny little dot.

I thought heaven was way up there. I had never flown in an airplane, but I thought it was strange no one caught a glimpse of those pearly gates midflight. I started to sing and made up a song about living on a dog cloud. I was told in several church services after an hour and a half of choir songs that "This is what heaven is like—endless singing. So get ready!" I loved singing for hours but was concerned we would all get a bit bored of it after a while, and then what? People-watch the people down below?

The hose got dislodged from the springs, and so I picked it back up, threaded it under the bar, up over the springs and onto the mat.

I came out here to think a lot, dream a lot. I wondered about the meaning of life and why pain exists if God made everything.

And why I couldn't be naked out here if God made this body of mine. Did Satan make it bad when Eve shamed us all with a single bite? And if God knew everything, didn't he know Satan was going to be a filthy cheat? So why even create him in the first place? And if we pray for our enemies, who exactly is praying for Satan? And just what would it feel like to kiss or to be naked with another person?

Existence, wonder, nakedness—this is what I sorted out on this black mat. I had rollerskated on it, slept on it, eaten on it, jumped in water on it, put my black Lab, Bonnie, on it (plus her puppies, poor things). My parents would spray us with the hose and laugh as we tried to avoid its coldness. Once, we situated this trampoline between the overhang of our house and the swimming pool so we could jump from the roof to the trampoline to the pool. I thought it was the best idea of our entire childhood. And I thought my parents were the best parents for allowing such life-threatening adventures. They watched, laughing at how high we could get or cheering with the extra flip at the end.

I smile when I think about this risky fun. I wondered why it couldn't always be this way—the good times.

I heard three voices yelling from the back window of our house. The deeper voice was angry, yelling fast and harsh. My mother was there too, trying to calm my sister. I heard my sister scream and I knew she was getting an "ass woopin'," as our dad called it. My whole body cringed and I wanted to save her but knew my intervention would only win me the same.

I knew how it all felt—the yelling and all the rest. I normally broke down crying before the belt hit because I'm the fragile one, the youngest of three, and a shy people-pleaser. I also knew how much that leather belt cracked and stung, so my crying beforehand was not an act but a soulful plea for mercy. My mother's weapon of choice was the wooden spoon. Needless to say, her spankings were preferable over my father's. She always gave me a second chance or pretended to spank me with the spoon as I let out fake cries so my siblings wouldn't think she was easy on me. She and I would stifle our giggles at each pretend outcry. I think my prespanking sobs made her have pity. Really, I think we were the same and she knew I broke right when she gave me the disappointed look.

I turned my body over and peered face-down through the woven mat. Water collected and hugged itself seconds before falling.

I don't think my parents knew how much it hurt to hear yelling and fights, to cover my ears and hum so I didn't hear the details. I assumed it was what all parents did—got sick of each other after a while.

I knew pieces of my parents' childhood. My father was sent away at nine years young to work for a family, and hasn't stopped working yet at seventy-two. He has parted his hair on the same side of his head since he came out of the womb—on the left.

My mother, a middle child, was curly-headed and taught to be what most 1950s American girls were taught to be—polite. She has the most beautiful dimple in her cheek when she smiles. She worked as a secretary to help put my father through college, then gave up her career to raise my brother, sister, and me. We were homeschooled before homeschooling was cool. She gave a lot to us. We've given her, in turn, her share of joy and yelling matches, hugs and stress.

I knew a lot of the good stuff about my parents' younger

years, but not much of the struggles. I think that's because there are truths that are hard to share.

I remember laying my head on my grandmother's lap and playing with her fake fingernails as she watched *MASH* on TV. Her nails were long, skin soft right at her fingertip. We didn't talk about anything deep as I lay there cuddled up to her. Mostly school, makeup, and her desire to perm my hair.

Grandpa was a quiet man, but as sweet as they come. He always let me play in their attic, and for some reason I can only picture him in an old blueish-gray work suit with a pocket on the left—his left, my right. I think I interpreted my grandparents' small talk to mean there was nothing complicated about their lives.

But she left them once—four boys and a husband.

She came back I'm not sure how many months later, and I think that explains a lot about my father. There are circumstances that leave marks on us and continue to leave marks on the ones we love if left unresolved. Divorce was threatened a lot in our house, and my assumption was that it was threatened in my parents' childhood more than mine. My brother, sister, and I were asked only twice who we wanted to live with. I never answered. And the question made me angry.

It just didn't make sense with all of the Sunday-best act. It felt fake. You could just sense that everyone else wanted to throw up their hands and admit they didn't have it all figured out. But no one wanted to give the first confession.

I knew my parents were trying, but the trying was leaving a mark on all of us, especially my mother. I felt like her protector, her advocate and safe spot within our home. She and I, we saw eye to eye on everything. My dad had to scoop me up in his arms for us to see eye to eye. He was tall in stature and short in temper. My favorite memories are of him turning on his record player and scooping me up to dance. Eventually he would put me down, grab my mother by the waist, and do the two-step. They'd dance in rhythm, then later fight in rhythm.

Right now, they were fighting in rhythm with my sister, poor girl. The arguing stopped, and I was glad, but I knew what the house would be for the rest of the evening—tense and cautious, the air healing up from a rough fight. I heard from the window, "This hurts me more than it hurts you," and thought, *I doubt it.* I let out a breath as the water dripped from my hair to my nose smashed on the mat. I saw Bonnie, our black Labrador, underneath, wet coated. She knowingly put her nose to mine.

I relaxed my body, then I stood and jumped high again, closed my eyes so my body could feel the free fall more vividly. We do that as children—close our eyes so our bodies see things.

I loved the good times, all the dancing and water fights and playing chase in the dark. I couldn't quite reconcile how there was so much fun but also so much anger, like a rollercoaster that makes you shout with joy on the uphill, then shriek in terror because it's just straight down and too fast. Families are often a mixed bag instead of just one thing. And so it's confusing to know just what is happening, just what is fun or too rough of a dance.

I wanted to feel safe and see things beyond this little spot I knew. Maybe I'd see the other side of the world someday, see how different other people's lives were from my tiny New Mexico town. Maybe I was here to stay.

I dropped to my back again and let the water pool, silvery ribbons hugging my body ever so slightly. The cloud dog was gone, just a blank blue space now.

Holy Rollers

I sat for hours in an orange overstuffed rocking chair, head adorned with my dad's giant silver headphones. My high-waist jeans and bowl haircut completed my '80s cool-kid vibe. I rocked back and forth while listening to old records, falling in love with the sound of music.

I can still hear the creaking of the rocking chair, feel the cloth-covered buttons of the upholstery on my back, feel how the chair enveloped my scrawny frame. "Footloose" played, and I rocked hard in rhythm. I did not yet know who Kenny Loggins was but would one day learn he wrote the song and said his matrimony vows nude with all of his nude guests. Now all I can think about when I hear his name is him and his wife walking down the aisle, wobbly bits out. I was warned not to listen to certain kinds of music. I could listen to "edifying" music like Evie, 4-Him, and Carman, and somehow the oldies were lumped into this category of safe and edifying.

I sat in that orange beast of a chair listening to anything I could. This is where I began to realize the power of music. It put me in a different world, spoke right to my soul.

It spoke not only words but emotion. It sent me on a journey of both transcendence of the body and also an inward look into my self. I thought it was interesting that people who claimed not to be musical still used music throughout their lives. When a baby was born, we sang to calm and to bond. On holidays, we sang to celebrate and to savor. On birthdays and in religious gatherings, we sang. When people married and died, again, we sang. So much of life was marked with songs, and I knew why—music connected us.

As the icon herself said, "Music makes the people come together."

Even though I agreed, as a child I wasn't allowed to listen to Madonna. I was told her clothes were too risque and that "no one should be singing about virgins being touched." I didn't know what a virgin was, nor did I know what "being touched" meant. Those conversations were off limits in our house, probably out of embarrassment or maybe in the hope that if the conversation wasn't happening, our bodies would remain sexually dormant until marriage.

I wasn't sure how a person like Madonna could be so right about music making the people come together, but so wrong to listen to.

So while other kids were listening to Madonna and the Beatles, I was listening to the golden oldies, Kenny Loggins, Evie, and inspirational religious groups. The orange chair was a magical spot in a place where I felt mismatched. We were a sports and physical labor family, not an artsy-fartsy one. So while my older brother and sister practiced basketball and any other sporty thing ever invented, I found myself in this chair or climbing high in the tree in our front yard to write poetry or songs.

Songs lingered up in those tree branches. I often felt like the trees had voices of their own. All I had to do was listen.

I revolved between four places—the trampoline, the trees, the piano, the orange chair. To me, that's all I needed, and there really wasn't much else in my town anyway.

Oh, Deming—one stoplight, one high school, one grocery store, zero Walmarts, one movie theater (until it burned down), metropolis.

Everyone knew our family for two reasons. First, everyone knows everyone in a small town like this one. Second, my dad has something I like to call big man syndrome. He's the boss of everyone. My father loves parties, bossing, and hardcore labor, and he loves his three children doing hardcore labor even more. We tore out a yard, wheeled off a small hill of rocks, installed a sprinkler system, planted a yard, changed the oil on our car, built fences, tore out floors, put in floors, remodeled a house, and worked in the chili fields.

When I was twelvish, he handed my brother, sister, and me each a tiny razorblade and told us to take the clear coat off of an old car he'd bought; we scraped an entire car with two-inch razors. I'm sure that was a waste of time, plus mildly dangerous.

Needless to say, I am quite different from my father. Needless to say, it doesn't go so well in the future when he meets my musician fiance with long fingernails made of clippings from ping pong balls (something only a music nerd does for better guitar tone).

But it was in a lot of those tedious jobs that I found myself making up songs—an entire storyline evolving each time. Me: the princess. My brother: my guide. My sister: the powerful feminist queen. We battled dragon-filled jungles, singing and waiting for my prince to rescue me from my workaholic father, who didn't let me watch cartoons on Saturday but instead made me weed a chili field. So music became my therapy early on. It would deepen and mold my life in ways I didn't know it could.

I was around ten years old when we pulled up in our ancient blue Oldsmobile. I examined the rough exterior of the building and the graffiti to the left. The front door was hard to open, but when it did, music came blaring out. Years ago the building was a bar. Later it was turned into a skating rink, and now it was a place the wild "holy rollers" met. A wild hippie friend of my mother's told us about it, so here we were.

In the early days, our family was nondenominational, then Baptist, then Methodist. I thought we went to church because that's what Americans did, even if you didn't believe in the whole shebang. We prayed without fail at the table each night, eyes closed and holding hands. It always felt so robotic, like brushing your teeth or tying your shoes. But it was necessary so our food wouldn't poison us. And it somehow felt comforting, this robotic daily rhythm. My Muslim friend across the street prayed before each meal as well. We once tried to save each other, told each other plainly in turn, "You know, you're going to hell because you believe in the wrong God." Our debate skills were severely lacking, because it wasn't even five minutes into the debate that our attention was diverted by making mud pies.

I always felt connected to something beyond myself, though I didn't find it at church. At church, I mostly counted the light fixtures, looked intently to see whether the architecture was symmetrical or asymmetrical, and drew in the hymnal. Once I drew a penis in a hymnal, or really, what I thought a penis would look like, because I had never seen one. I immediately erased it, though you could still see its indention clearly in the paper. So I just put a large scribble over top, praying to the Lord that no one would ever know I wondered about the male private parts. My dad liked the church we went to, but the rest of the family used the time for naps, so this is why we found ourselves parking our blue Oldsmobile by the curb and walking into what sounded more like a rock-and-roll-laden deliverance session than a church service.

As we walked into the bar church, a very friendly Mexican woman greeted us, then a man, then another woman. It seemed everyone was so excited to see us. It made me excited too. The interior was colorful with glittery flags on the walls, and colorful with the people who attended, unlike the mostly white church we had been sleeping in.

We found a spot in the back. The band played loud and fast. People swayed or rocked their bodies in rhythm, but most got out of their seats and danced wildly in the aisles or up front. It felt like we'd gone through a portal into a different world. We saw one man get on his belly and pretend to swim as they sang "Swimming in the River," which was really the old song "Rolling on the River" with new "holy" words.

Our stiff bodies were in stark contrast to all of the wild people dancing or swimming. Especially my dad. I think he felt that falling on the floor was uncouth—in general, and also in relation to his proper Baptist roots.

And then we saw them, the most dynamic duo of pastors ever to hit New Mexico. The woman was the epitome of loud—red lipstick, big hair, big smile—loud in voice, charisma, and fashion combined. The man looked kind and jolly as he did a little two-step shuffle around the podium. They were suit-wearing, praise-flag-waving Texans with extra large shoulder pads.

I saw a young girl dancing up front, and I wished I could feel so free in front of so many people. They weren't afraid of being in their bodies—dancing, moving, singing. I think my mother felt the same. A winning combo of culture and religion gave her the notion that women were in second place. I wondered what she thought about all of those strong-looking women dancing around. I think something inside of her lit up, something that she had tried to ignore for who knows how long.

This bar church was wild. I loved it immediately.

We walked out the door thanking people and smiling, piled into our old blue Oldsmobile. "What a bunch of holy rollin' radicals!" My dad laughed hard and waved his hands in the air like he had an imaginary hanky in one hand. I hung my arm out the window and just couldn't wait until next week to go again. I was in.

This wild church became my close tribe. We helped neighbors, visited orphanages. The pastors adopted a little girl and everyone cheered upon her arrival. I vacuumed the floors and washed the toilets, sang in the ensemble and taught Sunday school. We built a new building, and I did it all there as well. I "put my back into it," as my dad would say, though my dad wasn't too pleased with my church choice and continued to make fun of it with falling on the floor and shaking.

My mom and I were the only two who went. My sister and brother got scared away at different points. The whole rodeo was a little too wild for them. They didn't like the tongues-speaking or the dancing until midnight. Me, I went as much as possible, and the pastors became my second set of parents. I loved them deeply, trusted them fully. A trust that was gained because it felt like they really listened. They didn't push the kids away because of their youth; they didn't tell girls their voices didn't matter. They saw us. And they loved in the physical way—with pizza, tears, and presence.

I did think it was odd when I didn't feel well and was told I had a demon in my body. I thought a demon would feel a lot different than this. I supposed it was a mild demon, one of the nicer ones that give you a bellyache instead of cancer. Or when my sister was told she couldn't leave the building until she spoke in tongues.

I thought it was odd when my gay friend felt she was delivered from being gay. I wondered how a demon could attach itself to someone, force their attraction to the same sex against their will. I now wonder if she went along with it because she liked this wild church too and just hoped she could stay if she buried parts of who she was. There are things we suppress to be part of a tribe.

Though I loved my tribe, I had small questions about its ideology. But you couldn't really question authority figures. It was off limits. I think the questions would have implied that this godly authority figure didn't have all of the answers after all, and if that were true, the gig would be up, structures would collapse, and people would run wild in the streets, because if no one has all the answers, good Lord, what on earth will happen to us?

If you question, you get kicked to the sidelines, treated as a rebel doubter, someone trying to lead everyone astray. Looking back, I think my dad felt kicked. He didn't buy any of it. He would make fun of the whole thing, which made me mad and fueled my fire to go to church more. The church leaders told me I was being controlled by my dad. My dad told me they were controlling me. Two sides saying the same thing about the other. A common refrain. I'm sure they were both right about some things, wrong about others. But at the time, I thought you were either entirely right or entirely wrong, in or out, part of us or part of them. And I thought I was pretty lucky to belong to the right, the in, and the us.

A lot grew and a lot fell apart in that little town, and eventually, my whole family moved away. And after a decade of being gone, I drove back to our old red-brick house, and it felt like visiting a ghost. I just sat there staring from the street.

There was the brick-covered mailbox I hit with our car when I was sixteen. I never told my parents about this. I suppose they are just now finding out. You can still see the crack in the mortar today.

I saw my brother and me sitting at the piano and singing for hours. I saw my dad rocking me when I was sick, my mom tucking me in and staying beside me for hours.

There was the kitchen window I nervously sneaked out of. I was caught and grounded for three months. It's where my fifteen-year-old self clutched the phone and whispered to my older sister, "I had my first kiss! Eh, well, my lips really sting. Is it supposed to hurt?" It's where my dad, sister, brother, and I decorated our parents' room as a surprise for my mother with a new comforter patterned with mauve and teal paint smears.

It's where I held my mother as she cried and knew her thirty-year marriage was over.

I heard my parents fighting as I lay in bed right through that first window on the right. I was the only child at home at that point. I could no longer walk into my brother's or sister's room to distract myself with conversation or jokes.

There are intricacies I will never know about, opinions I formed about my parents based on my narrow perspective. None of us knows the whole truth about someone's life; we have only glimpses into them because the past is tricky. What I now know is life can turn on a dime, and sometimes there are onlookers to our worst moments, the moments we hate who we have become.

I had just gone to bed for the night in a room that used to be my sister's. I heard arguing, a loud noise. I felt our house shake. I heard someone run upstairs, so I followed and found my mother on her bed. I hugged her as she sobbed, my shirt becoming soaked through. Right there on the lovely mauve and teal comforter, we both knew it was over.

I was pulled out of school the next day. I remember sitting on the stairs at high school waiting for someone to pick me up. I thought it was unnecessary. I was sent to my pastors' house, and I cried for two hours in their spare bedroom. They thought I was napping, but I didn't let on otherwise. I'm not exactly sure why. It all felt sort of hazy and too sad to correct anything.

We had a court date the following week, and I just wasn't sure how a daughter was supposed to testify about her parents. I looked into the eyes of all of these people. They all wanted me to dish, tell all of the awful secrets I knew.

But I didn't want to tell them anything. How could I tell the bad and exclude all of the good? Both of my parents tucked me in. Both of them said prayers for me. I loved them both and knew they loved me. It's a mixed bag, was I supposed to tell that? And was this finally my moment to talk about *all* of it? The young boys, the church leader who told me to leave my clothes on the floor? How do you tell a judge the whole truth when you don't even know it yourself? I saw things. I heard things that

I was still trying to figure out. I looked from my father to my mother. They fixed their eyes on mine and wondered what I was about to do.

Their eyes were fixed on me like when I was a kid on our trampoline and they waited in anticipation for my next brilliant trick. I jumped, flipped, landed awkwardly. But this time there was more at stake, and no one applauded after the performance. I left feeling that I had betrayed everyone. Some of my parents' friends were there. Some of them hugged me, but I just wanted them to leave me alone. I smiled instead. Acted collected. I wanted to go hide. I wanted to go to the piano and let all of my confusion and sadness spill out. I wanted my parents to stay together but was also glad when they divorced. I loved life, knew I had a purpose, and knew I was loved. And at times I also just wanted to run or be rescued by Jesus breaking through those clouds as I lay on that trampoline again and again.

And so this is where I begin—comfort and love mixed with pain and anger all in one family, one little town. I begin with learning that there are tribes that divide people politically, religiously, physically. I learn which tribe I belong to—conservative, Republican, Christian. I am born into circumstances with a hunger to know just what all of this is and what it all means.

I begin like a lot of people do—in a family, in a hometown. On a dot.

I Met a Boy

**I am a friend of God, I am a friend of God,
I am a friend of God, he calls me friend.**

—"LOVE OF MY LIFE," MICHAEL GUNGOR
AND ISRAEL HOUGHTON

Here's the "meet cute" in a romantic comedy. Although this isn't only comedy but also drama, tragedy, total crazy town, and everything in between. It starts with a boy, a girl, and a practice room.

The first two times I saw him, we didn't really meet. The first time: he was romping around on a stage playing guitar at a church, unruly curly hair jutting out in every direction from underneath a backward beret.

What a weird guy, I thought.

The second time: a year later, I walked into a coffee shop as a freshman in college, and there he was, sitting in a chair in the corner, reading a book. He looked up and his eyes fixed on mine; it gave me chills. I grabbed my hot chocolate, then walked out of the coffee shop with my friends, acting cool and collected, though I was completely and happily unnerved.

The actual meet: I was on campus. I hung up an orange pay phone that was caked with a little grossness. I turned and there stood two guys in front of me. With a wide, warm smile, his friend Dan introduced us. "Hi, I'm Michael," Michael said. He shook my hand and looked me right in the eye for that "longer than normal" amount of time. They asked if I could join them for food. I told them I was sorry but I had to rush out for music practice. Months later Michael will tell me he was glad I was into music and that he had really liked my eyes.

The next time I saw him was across the student parking lot. Michael and Dan were in a full-on sprint when they saw me.

"You want to go eat pancakes at my parents' house?" Michael yelled in my direction, still sprinting. It was an unconventional approach.

"No, but thank you!" I yelled back.

He called once. I couldn't place him at first. He asked if we should get together with friends. I said no.

This guy, he was as persistent as they come. He took a no as a "just see if you can catch me." One day, he tagged along when a friend asked me to coffee. I was surprised to see Michael, then surprised how I forgot my friend was even there, because the chemistry with Michael was electric.

I had recently broken up with my hometown sweetheart, and I wasn't looking for someone else, so we didn't exchange phone numbers and our paths didn't cross for a month. One night I was talking with some friends after a school event and Michael walked by three times before acting like he bumped into me. (This mild form of stalking is cute if you like the guy, creepy if you don't. I happened to kind of like the guy.)

"Oh! Hey." He smiled big, acting surprised to see me.

"Hi!" I paused.

We stood there just nodding and smiling, both waiting for the other to say something.

"So . . . when are you going to play me the songs you wrote?" he asked.

"Oh, yeah, um, well . . . I don't know," I said, a little embarrassed.

"How about now?" he asked.

I think I surprised both of us when I said okay, and we headed to the rehearsal rooms on campus. I sat on the piano bench, and he sat on the floor by the door with his Olsen guitar. We sang for hours. I remember watching him close his eyes while he sang. It was like music was as easy as talking for him. It was my turn, and I felt like a child showing Van Gogh her notebook sketches filled with scribbles and mistakes. But he liked my songs anyway or maybe just pretended so we could keep being with each other. I think we both really liked being in a room together with the door closed. It was quite the Christian flirt show—two extremely religious kids playing songs to each other about how much they love God and feeling things my mother would deem "the traps of Satan."

We eventually ran out of songs, so we jumped in his green Neon and he took me to the same coffee shop I first saw him in. We played Connect Four while sitting in front of a fire—probably the most sexually charged game of Connect Four in history. Then we jumped back in the Neon, and he took me to his parents' house. Bold move. We were talking in the driveway when he asked if I knew how to swing dance.

"Nope."

"Can I teach you?"

I held my breath as he took my hand. We both smiled way too big the whole time. It was one of those magical nights that leave you dizzy.

He was wildly adventuresome and cared only about jazz music. I thought that was weirdly charming. The only person I knew who listened to jazz was my grandfather.

Weeks later at a park, it began raining so hard everyone ran to their cars in a craze. But he and I hunkered together on a swing in a gazebo for protection. The storm was so harsh the wind threw rain into the gazebo from every side. We laughed and screamed as rain soaked us. I felt him pull me close, his hand slowly moving right into mine and holding it tight.

Jesus was the center of it all for both of us. Before Michael, I dated Jesus at one point. It's a thing young Christian girls did back in the day to have a pure life. I'm pretty sure Jesus was dating lots of other girls at the same time, but no one ever acknowledged the weirdness of that. I also never heard any boys say they were dating Jesus.

So as I was dating Jesus and a handful of other boys through high school, Michael wasn't dating anyone. He had never kissed a girl except for once in high school when he kissed his first Jesus-dating girlfriend on the hand, a scandalous move that compelled her parents to tell them to "slow things down." He was about as pure as they come. He led music at his dad's church, and a month into our relationship, he asked me to sing with him—the start of our musical duo adventures.

I ran up the stairs in my dorm after one of our wild romantic nights, barely making curfew. *Curfew*, in college—a perk for just the girls. I called my mom to talk about this wonderful new life I was creating and this boy I was falling for. I knew she would be so excited. We missed each other so much, talked as much as possible.

"You won't believe how funny he is, and it's like he is really listening to me . . . and he has so many interesting things to say. And he sings—he plays guitar and writes songs like me, can you believe it? And we sat on top of this bulldozer, isn't that so funny? . . . it was great. We ran in the rain . . . so fun. He is Puerto Rican . . . bonus."

There was a long pause as I held the phone. I checked to see if she was still there.

"A lot of boys sing and play the guitar," she said at last, unimpressed.

"But . . . but he is amazing . . . and . . . and he leads music at his dad's church!" I said, hoping that would be the winning ticket.

"A lot of guys seem amazing; a lot of guys lead music," she said.

I was confused. I thought she would be so excited. I went on and told her about their church. Again, she was unimpressed.

I wasn't sure what turned this conversation so sour, but I found out she wasn't the only one upset. So were the home-town pastors; so were other friends. While in college, and while dating Michael, I was helping with music at a church my little hometown church was connected to. I didn't know going to two churches was a no-no. I found out going to a different place was not only frowned upon but forbidden. I thought going to two places was pretty fun and extra-Christian. I had no idea they would be upset, and I didn't know a place could own a person. That's when I learned that some pastors blame other pastors for "stealing their sheep," and suddenly I felt like I was in some cult, but without the matching haircuts. I pushed the feeling aside—no, it's not control; they just must not understand, or maybe I'm wrong and actually doing something bad.

I held the phone, not sure what to say to my mom—a foreign thing for her and me. I could hear her breath and I knew she was tired. She had just gone through a painful divorce after a thirty-year marriage. She was hurting. Plus, her darling daughter was falling for a boy she didn't even know in a state miles away in a town with more than one stoplight. I felt so much sadness for her and wanted to wrap her up, tell her I'd do whatever she needed. I just wanted her to be happy.

Instead we hung up the phone in tension, and for the first time in my life, I felt differently than my mother. It was an unsettling experience for both of us. I always wondered what she went on to after that conversation. All I could do was sit blankly.

I wanted to run home and hug her, tell her, "Look! I'm good, the other church is good—see?!" I wanted to go back to my old church, go back to the safe hometown I knew just to avoid the stress and be back "in." I wanted everyone back home to know I was not just good but great! *I'm not straying! See?! I can still speak in tongues!*

I loved this mother of mine so thoroughly. I saw all she gave up for me, all she continued to give. This transition had to be hard on her. It was definitely hard on me. So I tried to give Michael up, to break up with him and remain part of the hometown team.

I remember sitting in Michael's car and being pretty worked up about the whole thing. I told him I was so sorry but it just couldn't work out. We were like Romeo and Juliet, but the religious version. Our two worlds wouldn't let us be together. Oh, the drama. We had to break up.

But like the episode of *Seinfeld* where George won't let his girlfriend break up with him (I love this episode), Michael wouldn't let me break up with him. I was aghast.

"Um, you can't not accept a breakup; it's not a thing you can do," I said firmly with tears still wet on my face.

"But . . . you like me, right?" he asked matter-of-factly.

"Right."

"So you are breaking up with me because of your mother, right?"

"Yeah, it's just, I love her and don't want to hurt her. And she doesn't like you very much. She kind of hates you."

"But . . . you like me?"

"Yeah, I do."

"Well . . . doesn't that seem strange? You should probably go with your heart, not what someone else wants for you. What do *you* want?"

I remember looking at him and slightly laughing at his simple question. I broke up with three guys before Michael, and with each breakup, the guy walked away with slumped shoulders and a wounded heart. But not this guy. He didn't slump; he refused. He told me he was in it as long as I was. I dried my eyes and laughed at the absurdity of our situation—my tribal reasons, his simple question. We remained silent for a long time in his little Neon. People walked by. I thought about what I wanted.

"Okay, I'm in it," I said.

Michael and I started spending every moment of free time together, and I stopped telling my mother about it. Maybe ignorance *was* bliss. We continued our wild adventures during the day, then at night the girls in my dorm wanted me to dish on what Michael and I were doing physically. But all I could say was, "Well, he kissed my neck hard, like *reeeeally* hard!" Which is way more uncomfortable than sexy and can sometimes block the windpipe. We did this because we made a rule we wouldn't kiss on the lips until we knew we loved each other, reasoning that the cheeks and neck were more pure than the lips. The lips were serious. The lips meant "we are going toward marriage and a mortgage and babies." My mother didn't even know I had kissed someone on the lips before. She wanted me to wait until my wedding day, and I felt like a wretched floozy for giving my first kiss away at fifteen, then jean jammin' at seventeen.

Michael and I, we just kept it real clean with kissing only on the cheek or neck for hours in our university's parking lot, giving each other red chapped faces. Years later, I heard stories of how people could clearly see us in that parking lot and wondered why we dodged each other's lips so much. It's embarrassing to think about.

We listened to more jazz. We rollerbladed '80s style. We flew kites. One day we sat in the grass while he told me he loved me, and I hesitated to really consider and also to give dramatic pause. I think it scared him.

"I love you too," I said finally.

"I guess this means I can really kiss you now."

I laughed. "You aren't supposed to say that. You're just supposed to kiss."

It was an absurdly perfect moment, and we were absurdly over-the-top in love. Then we raced to his parents' house and told them, "We finally kissed each other!"

His entire family cheered and danced around the house. I didn't know a single person who would race home to tell their parents about a first kiss, let alone whose parents would cheer about it—I liked these people. And I felt I was somehow winning big—me, this small-town girl somehow finding this amazing guy who had this amazing family, and maybe life would be amazing from here on out. I knew my mother and friends would soon see how amazing it all was. I just needed to give it time.

Time crept slowly. I remember when she walked into my cramped dorm room. The room was big enough for two twin beds and two tiny desks. It always smelled of old Chinese food, because I was always eating old Chinese food. She was one of my best friends from my hometown. I knew she had been having a difficult time here at college, so I figured she wanted to talk about it. Instead, out came something entirely different. "Um. My dad called and he told me I can't be your friend anymore."

I stared at her. I thought it was a joke and I sort of laughed. But she continued, saying that the four of us who came to this school from our hometown had been forbidden to attend a different church. I was the only one who didn't obey this command, and so she had to end our friendship. I sat on the bed in confusion. We had been friends since childhood. I had no idea how to respond. I sat there wondering how we were even having this conversation when she got up and calmly left.

I was overcome with anxiety and guilt. I thought my heart must be so filthy and rotten that I couldn't see what was right. I wracked my brain relentlessly, trying to find the thing that made me rotten, the thing that made this boy and this church I liked rotten as well. But I couldn't find anything. Well, there was all the neck kissing, then lip kissing. I immediately repented.

Days later I received a letter from my hometown pastors, my

second parents. I unfolded the crisp paper and read the lines. It said I was no longer following God and that they would no longer send me fifty dollars per month to help with school. It was short, to the point, with two sentences and signed like a business letter. I couldn't believe what I was reading. Though I had very little money, I didn't care about the fifty dollars. I only cringed with shame. I wondered what was being said about me, what lies they must have heard, because I would have expected a letter like that to come if I were yelling and tripping small children or had become a wild vagrant spreading violence in the streets . . . or cursing, but I didn't curse. Surely this wasn't in response to dating a boy they didn't like. Or going to a second church.

I cried in secret about these things. I didn't tell a soul about my lost friendships or the letter. I didn't even tell Michael until years later. I thought I actually was doing something wrong and deserved to be punished. I wondered if I was blind. Maybe Michael was one of those wolves in sheep's clothing I heard so much about. Maybe the hometown tribe was the ultimate authority in my life and I was never supposed to trust myself. Maybe my heart was rotten so I couldn't see that it was leading me into a terrible place. But my heart felt open. It felt good, so I really wasn't sure what to do about the letter or my ex-friend or my mother.

I had this tribe I gave my life to pulling hard one way, and my heart pulling me elsewhere. I didn't understand how they couldn't see what I saw. It was like I was seeing the color blue and they were seeing red.

What I just couldn't see then was that it wasn't about my heart; it was about my obedience to authority, my submission to the tribe. I didn't follow the rules. I hadn't even known they existed until now. It felt like *The Twilight Zone*, because I saw this happen to other people, and I always thought terribly of *those people*. I thought they really must have fallen into the deep end, strayed far. And now it was me, but I wasn't straying from religion; I was straying from my tribe. I had always heard about cultic tendencies like that, but I never would have imagined that the church I so loved would have that tendency. I never thought I would be one of those people who just couldn't see the control, even when it came in black-and-white print on cardstock—signed, even.

After years of entrusting someone else to make your decisions, it can feel dangerous to start making them for yourself.

In seven brief months, the rift between my mother and me, my dot and me, became a chasm, a deep unbridgeable thing. I was quickly wrung out and confused. Michael was persistent, fought for me, told my mother what he thought, and no one had done that with her. She disliked him even more.

There was one night when the tension peaked. It started with a tangled story of sneaky lies and ended with my mother telling me she was done with me; I was going to hell. I was told to pack my bags and come home. College would be taken online, if at all. I couldn't understand it. Just how did we get here? A mother and daughter going from seeing everything the same way to seeing each other as a threat. It made me remember when I held her on that mauve bedspread, back when we were on the same side.

I made matters more tense. I didn't pack my bags and go home. I called my father, told him how things had unraveled, asked him to help me with college tuition for the rest of the semester, and told him I'd pay him back. This must have cut my mother deeply. I had called the person who had wounded her the most. It felt like a betrayal. And I was ashamed of myself. But it seemed like if I went back home, I would buy back in to the control of the tribe and never leave again.

I finished the semester with bruises. My mom and I weren't talking. I thought my life was at a crossroads, and I felt that no matter which road I chose, I was leaving someone I loved behind. I felt the dot I had come from shaking me loose, but I wanted to cling to it, cling to everything that felt safe and familiar. I also wanted to run toward my future, my own ideas about life, but it was scary to leave what I had known.

So I decided to escape. I packed up my bags, my dorm room, broke up with Michael, and moved to Arizona.

I thought if I could just get away for a while, I could get a breath and make a decision from a place of centeredness instead of this chaotic mixture of pure excitement with Michael and confusion with my roots.

I took a job organizing inventory in a fancy department store and was amazed at the calm. This tedious kind of work felt good, somehow therapeutic. I worked this job and another at a clothing store to pay for classes and rent.

I spent countless hours working overtime, organizing cups, crystal vases, food processors. I would go home and sit at the piano, then study, then go to class, sleep in my shared one-bedroom apartment, then back to hours in the department store ordering fancy china for people who had more money than they knew what to do with. But in between all of those things, I found I was learning to tune out the clashing voices in my life and learning to trust myself.

On a few weekends, I drove to see my mother. I felt it was necessary. She did grow me, was cut right through her belly for me, then fed me from that very body. That's a whole lot of work in itself. We reached for each other in little ways to help the chasm grow smaller. But it was difficult because she was still on the dot, and I was being shaken off.

A semester had passed when one day my roommate told me to get dressed and wait in our apartment. It was my birthday, and there was a surprise coming.

I heard a steel-stringed guitar being played outside the kitchen window. I smiled to myself on the sofa. I knew that sound and that voice. I ran to the window, and there stood Michael, smiling and singing. He had driven from Texas to Arizona as a birthday surprise.

His way of showing love was the wild kind—not worried about doing something absurd for a person. He was young and fearless and I ate up all the sappiness of young love. I stopped second-guessing myself, trusted that this was part of the direction I wanted to go in. He told me he was still in love with me, and he had only eight hours until he had to drive back to school. So we made out.

Months later at the absurdly green age of nineteen, I found myself saying yes to a proposal on a hilltop in San Francisco. We called to tell our families at a pay phone on the Golden Gate Bridge. Most of them were happy. My dad was a little hesitant, but happy. My mother responded with a mixture of disbelief and suppressed rage.

PART 2

LINE

Imagine one day your dot starts to tremble. You never knew it could. It shakes and tips to the side, sending you sliding to the edge holding on for dear life. You shake your fist and demand that your dot be calm. It obeys. But the next day it shakes again. Again you command your dot to be still, but it doesn't listen this time. You cry and beg your dot to be good to you like it promised it would from the start, but the begging seems to cause more shaking. Your dot turns more, thoroughly shakes you loose.

Strangely, gravity has shifted. You are a bit dizzy, but as you look up and brush yourself off, you see a line beneath your feet, stretching out for miles. You are scared because you don't know this line. You look at its edges. They are blurry, undefined. You wobble, gain balance, take one step. Then two. Then three. Like a toddler, you learn how to walk, then run, on this line. ,

You turn your head to see the dot behind you, realize with a jolt that it never was a dot. It was just the bird's-eye view of this line. You had to change your perspective to see it. The change is frightening, as change always is, but you do like the perk of more leg room, more expansiveness.

Some of your friends are still living on their dots. You tell them about your line, but they have never heard of that before, so they scratch their heads and think you must be losing it.

You are thankful for your line, and you ask it to keep you safe and never shake like that mean dot did.

Where the Light Comes In (Part 2)

It's true how they say it feels like time slows. It felt like an hour had passed, but the nurse had just spoken the words; it was minutes, really. I looked to Michael, wondering whether we had both heard the same thing. She was still talking, explaining other things—our baby was blue, she didn't have enough oxygen, she would be taken for tests . . . The world spun.

I watched people hurry around a baby our culture treats differently from moment one. She wasn't what they had expected either.

Like a drunk trying to convince a police officer she is sober, I nodded to the nurse—yes, I'm okay, I understand, I'm totally listening even though the whole world is spinning. I remember Michael's face. We locked eyes, gave each other a slight smile, a kind of heartbroken smile, one I hadn't ever seen on his face before. He was trying to be strong for me. He held my hand tight. But I could see the helplessness that took him.

The only stories I had heard of children with DS were of loss or intense difficulty. I held a friend's beautiful baby girl a few years ago right on Christmas Day. We sang Christmas songs as the oxygen tank hissed in rhythm, the canula threading through her doll-sized pjs and into the tiniest nose I had ever seen. She had Down syndrome and heart complications. She lived for a year, then passed away, and I didn't know how her parents got through it. The thought made me cave in. Would our girl die? Or survive and face a lifetime of surgeries and complications, alive but struggling? I couldn't bear it.

We had no words. We just held hands as the first wave hit, worried that more were coming.

When I was pregnant with our first daughter, the doctor told us there were little signs. "These may be signs of Down syndrome or they may fade and be nothing." I remember talking on the phone to my mother in our back yard. "Well, if she does have it, we'll love her just the same," I said confidently and proudly. And now, now that we were in the hospital being told the diagnosis of our second baby's condition, I was shocked at myself, my lack of confidence and calm. I couldn't believe I was so sad; I hadn't thought I would be. I'd thought I was so different from everyone else. News like this was always given to other people, and so I thought I was such an enlightened person with such a positive attitude toward the whole thing.

And now my plans were changed. I had made plans for this little girl without even laying eyes on her—plans for her future, how she would fit into *our* lives; plans for her relationship with her older sister, how they would run through the hall—*Her feet are folded up. Will she ever run?*—how they would whisper under the covers—*Will Lucie talk? Will she live?*—how they would fall asleep under the frayed needlepoint girls in the yellow frames. Now all of that was gone, and it unlatched thoughts I never knew I was capable of.

They gave her some medicine, did some tests. They wrapped her up and carefully handed her back to me. "Let's see if she can nurse before she is off to her echocardiogram."

She looked up at me. She had skin, fingers, eyes—I thought there was supposed to be more of a difference. I loved her so, and I was terrified of nursing her because I knew it would bond us even more, and then I'd lose her.

But something shifted as I felt her body on mine. Whatever is in me that can really see—not my eyes but something else—unfolded and felt her, heard her communicating without words. She began nursing. I couldn't believe it. I could tell it was difficult for her. She tired quickly. We just lay there together—I, looking at her; she, blurry eyed and almost melting right into me. It felt like she was made to fit right here on my body, just this way. "I love you, sweet girl," I whispered and laid my face onto hers. She needed more nutrients, so she was given other milk, and something in me closed again. *My body can't give her what she needs. I'm failing her.* A kind nurse came and took her away; I worried again. I worried I couldn't control any of this and my girl wouldn't be mine much longer.

Was she ever really mine? Was this entire life ever really mine? Was my control all an illusion? I think so, but letting go of control isn't instant and wonderful. Sometimes it gives us rope burns as we slide down trying to hold on like a madman.

We had tried so long, had had an adoption fall through, and now here we were in the hospital room waiting for news—life or the other thing? I'd thought the waiting and fighting would reward us with the healthiest, non-crying, non-screaming baby that had ever lived. I'd thought this life was controllable, transactional. I'd bought right in to the illusion because I was a madman too.

Certainty and American Confessions

If you think you know what your life will look like in the future, it will look nothing like that.

—Twentieth Century Women

I watched each fairy tale again and again—the prince rescued the princess, and in the end was a wedding, always a wedding, with a perfectly timed, closed-mouth kiss. Ah, Prince Charming, your wonderfully chiseled chin and tight butt became so many children's secret love and coveted future.

I took my flowers and Father's arm, and we walked in pace toward Michael, my half–Puerto Rican prince wearing a tux and flip flops. It felt as if the rest of the world were at a standstill. We took each other's hands, made promises, exchanged rings. We released into the air the butterflies my mother gave us, symbolizing the new life our vows made. All fell straight to the ground; apparently someone had put them on an ice cooler before the wedding and they froze. Poor little guys. But suddenly one rose out of the ice cold clutches of death, and we cheered that sole survivor.

We sealed the deal with a slow passionate kiss, making some people squirm in their seats and some clap with excitement. "I now present to you Mr. and Mrs. Michael Gunnn-gooorrr!" Said very elongated and exuberantly. People cheered, and we danced back down the aisle holding tightly to each other.

I had found my soul mate. We had truth in our hands, certain of everything. Nineteen years young and so certain. We ran straight toward life like it was an adventuresome line beneath our feet, no longer a confining dot. I had the freedom to stay up late, eat Captain Crunch if I so desired. I could say Christianized curse words and have God-approved sexy time.

It's crazy to think that two years after we sang in that little practice room, we said "I do." Three years later, we sang to thirty thousand people in an arena and traveled the entire world together. Ten years later, we had our first daughter and our hearts exploded with love. Fourteen years later, we sat in a hospital room singing to a baby covered in wires and tubes, hoping she would wake up.

We had no thought that the faith we lived and breathed would one day lead us to the absence of it. No thought that our love for each other would bend under the weight of life. No thought that our lives would hold anything but this bliss.

Our first apartment is a tiny one in a new complex built on Riverside Drive. We are given an old sofa and a rocking chair. We buy a folding table to eat on and are given Michael's parents' old mattress. After installing it, they joyfully inform us that every one of their children was conceived on that well-worn sex pad—information I do not need.

My mother helps us arrange furniture and plans to guard our apartment against my prank-addicted family when we leave for our honeymoon. My mother rubs Michael's back as we pick up our suitcases and head to the door. He and I raise our eyebrows and smile like we aren't sure whether she is going to keep rubbing his back or stab him.

It was during our engagement that my mother began to love Michael, a definite turn from hanging up on him countless times. She was beginning to accept my decisions, a turn from giving my things away to Goodwill after a fight.

The turning point came when a single person inside my childhood tribe gave Michael her holy stamp of approval. She was a pastor my mother and I had both known for more than a decade. She had authority bias on her side. But I also think it came from the day I stood between Michael and my mother as they yelled at each other. I yelled louder: "You have to love each other because I love you both! And you'll be stuck with each other for a really long time, so stop the crazy!" They both kind of hushed and we all stood there awkwardly.

And now my mom makes him uncomfortable with all of the back rubs and lying in our bed in the morning to chat with us. I don't think she remembers what can happen to guys' anatomy in the morning, especially a guy who has saved all his sexy time for marriage.

We receive a very good job offer from a very large fancy church, and two months later we pack up our rocking chair and folding table, plus ancient sex pad, and move from the Panhandle State to the Mitten State.

We quickly cozy into marital-life patterns—get up, breakfast, work, school, sing at the fancy church with ten thousand people, then collapse at home at the end of a long day and think how fun it is to come home as married people. We buy a dog, a new bed to replace the ancient sex pad, and a wooden table to replace the broken folding one. We feel we have won the lottery with our perfect, holy relationship, his job, a new house, this quaint Dutch town—all of this at twenty years old.

Our family is proud, but even more, my mother is, and it feels so good after living in the bowels of hell for so long. She sees how connected Michael and I are, sees this shiny job Michael has landed, sees us playing music together, and it all makes her smile big. I thought we had this sort of life because we did all the right things to get here. I paid my dues by standing up for my beliefs in high school, giving my money away, fighting for our love, and only making out with Michael instead of doing the forbidden "no pants dance." I think life is like a transaction—we are good, so good things are finally happening to us. Fi-nal-ly . . . after twenty whole years. (I know, I know, I had a lot to learn.)

We talked about this transaction in a back yard as we watched the embers burn and tiny pieces of glowing ash float into the night sky. The Michigan air was crisp. There were always the same faces around the fire, and the conversations always started and ended the same—absurd, straight to existential. I was in art school, and while Michael held down the full-time job, we began traveling a little bit to play music. I felt my life consisted of two different worlds of people—the "secular lost people" and the "religious." I told stories about school, about one girl's sculpture of a dozen vaginas splayed in the lobby, some on their period. My church friends' eyes widened; my art-school friend laughed hard and cheered for feminine empowerment.

We were all young with budding dreams—two couples, five singles. We abandoned our Christian curse words for the regular ones around this fire and also abandoned any restraining of questions. Ben from Australia inevitably would say something about crawling through the brush and stabbing an alligator, making us all raise our eyebrows as if we had a psycho-killer in our midst. Kaley would tackle Ben, do a flip that ended with her standing on his shoulders, and then they'd wrap their bodies around each other. They always had to be touching. It was cute and gross. Jadranka the Croatian would go off on a tangent about how things were done in her country, and couldn't we Americans get over our ridiculous American pride already? "Why the 'h-e-double-hockey-sticks' do they have a giant American flag hanging behind the entire stage at church?" (She spelled out all of her curse words. Apparently God preferred it.) This would send us into the debate about how our country was built on the backs of slaves, with violence and genocide, and did our Bible support slavery? And then we would all question whether what we had known to be true was actually true or simply cloaked in tradition.

After we covered light topics like genocide, we dove into sexism, eternity, and this idea of a guy in the sky ruling things from up above. If God was good, why did some people have stories of immaculate healing but others died poor and starving? I told them about my younger self and a book on tape—oh yeah, *tape*. It was the new see-through kind. You could watch as the tape wound from one side to the other, and I was thrilled with this cutting-edge technology. I listened to it with my mother as we drove with the windows down in our old blue Oldsmobile.

The man talking on the see-through tape explained how he had died and gone to heaven. He saw a warehouse of sorts, filled with body parts—feet, knees, eyes, privates, all replacement parts for people down below. He didn't really say "privates," but I assumed there were privates and wondered what a man's private part would look like sitting on a shelf. The man said that in order to receive a body part, one has to pray and not sin between the time of pickup and delivery. And that could be a while, because after your angel picks up the body part, a war between angels and demons ensues on your angel's way back to earth. If you sin, your angel turns around, heads back to the warehouse, and the part gets restocked on the shelf.

So as a kid, I prayed, and if my prayer wasn't answered, I ran circles in my mind trying to figure out how I'd sinned. It was probably the curse word I said in my head. I should have just said it aloud if it counted anyway. Or maybe it was because I liked to watch people kiss on TV. I was supposed to close my eyes, but I squinted instead because I liked it. I thought most boys probably didn't get their prayers answered because they masturbated; their angels never stood a chance.

This see-through tape was my lens for faith. I remember feeling an ideology forming: If you are good, God gives you stuff. If you are holy enough, have enough faith, you get favor, blessings, health, a nice car, and a big bank account. It was all transactional. God was this guy in the sky giving things to the sinless and taking from the sinners. Sometimes speaking, some-times silent, making us flail with prayers about which road to take, which college to go to, which shirt to wear—God forbid the tight one makes a guy stumble. You'd hate to be the reason Joe didn't get that new foot.

This transactional idea followed me all the way into the back yard in Michigan. We laughed about the warehouse of body parts idea. But even though we didn't now believe there was a literal storage house, I realized this was how my tribe had been speaking all along, even now. Everyone still believed in superstition and gods raining blessings on the good people down below, giving health and wealth to the ones who shared this garbage version of the gospel. I probably would have said I had learned better by then, but belief is interesting. As I heard Peter Rollins once say, we don't know what we believe; it shows up in symptoms.

I never recognized my symptoms: fear, shame, constant need for acceptance. I probably would have told you that I was free and strong. But I remember conversations when sexism was laughed at, when women were treated like issues to be handled. Like in choir rehearsal in Michigan one night, one of the leaders told the women with big breasts to tape them down; men didn't need to see them wobble about. Everyone laughed. "And if you walk out of your house and you think you look good, gurrrrl, you better go change!"

The choir roared with laughter. Some of the women said it hurt to tape them, or that theirs bounced no matter what. "Well, then you'll just have to sit still or sit out." Everyone laughed again. I remember looking around bewildered; it felt so dehumanizing. You have to sit out because the body you were given moves in "unholy" ways when dancing in church? It seemed like women were cursed with these wonderful things to feed their babies, cursed because they caused men to stumble all over themselves to the extent that women were told to sit out. I wondered whether a guy had ever been told to tape his stuff down.

Men and women weren't allowed to sit in a car together at this church, or have a meeting together alone.

One time an assistant pastor was asked the question, "So how do you and your wife work something out if you can't see eye to eye on it?"

"Well, I win," he said simply. "I'm the man, so obviously I win the discussion."

It was strange to see such love in one area and oppression in another. The lead pastors were two of the most generous people I have known, extending love to Michael and me plus countless others.

I thought about these episodes around our fire pit. Someone kicked the logs and sparks went flying.

It brought up other memories, memories I had never thought about twice before now. About body shame and ignored abuse. One time my married friend told someone that one of the married pastors was hitting on her. No one believed her. They thought a guy like him (sucessful, Caucasian, power man) would never like a girl like her (poor, Croatian, "nobody"). And it was probably her fault he was looking at her because her breasts were big—tape 'em down.

It is sobering to think back on these early marriage stories and also ones of my childhood and teenage years. I feel they are insignificant—other people have faced worse horrors, so really, I should be quiet and move on. Then I remember how long I carried those stories in shame, how long it took me to realize I didn't need to carry it. Shame didn't die until I finally decided to see the oppressive system for what it was and not subject myself to it any longer. My stories were not like many other terrible stories I know. But just how dehumanizing does a thing need to be before you can say it out loud?

It is interesting what humans will subject themselves to because of tribalism or fear of being rejected. We all want to belong somewhere, and we know how the powerful can push.

Those nights by the fire made me wonder what I was building with my life, just what I was subscribing to. Did I think success was in standing in the lights in front of TV cameras, and if so, why did I believe that? It was exciting, absolutely. It felt amazing to make Jesus cool, but was that what he was really after? I felt like I had come from such an insignificant dot on a map and was now storing up a lot of pride in all of the fancy things I had managed to land. Sometimes people asked for pictures or autographs after a service or out-of-town show, and it really did a number on my ego. *You want a picture? Oh, now I must be somebody!* I liked it. It made me feel important, which was a definite turn from feeling so out of place growing up. I saw this Christian celebrity thing happening to me, and though I tried to push the feeling away, I wanted that stardom. I loved helping people, showing them they were loved, but I also wanted applause for that. I wanted to belong and feel important in the world, like I myself had done something for the good of all humanity. It's like my body began needing more of it. I thought it would make me feel complete, but then I started feeling cynical, sick in the heart. I needed more, more, more.

I looked at the fire and felt "this isn't me; this isn't who I want to be." I had let my once soft and open heart grow cynical and calloused. Though I sure would have loved to point a finger, I knew this wasn't anyone's fault but my own. I had really gotten caught up in the whole American dream. Don't get me wrong—I don't think having things is bad. But you can have things and possess nothing, or have things and possess them all. The second will ruin anyone.

I overheard some people talking about a community that met in a crappy building down the road, how the building was so bad because they gave all of their money away. They said the pastor spoke about love so much he was on the verge of heresy. This made me want to go, so I went alone and sat in the back. It was around Christmastime. I listened to two men speaking about Hanukkah, its history, its meaning. Then we sang a song that said "open hands are better than bombs are," and I remember giggling to myself in amazement that a church would sing about bombs. I thought all Christians were conservative Republicans, and I thought all Republicans liked war. And the song was a little wordy, didn't have the pop hook in the chorus. I liked the lack of spotlights and concrete and started sneaking off after playing music at our fancy church—what a rebel. You know someone is deep in the religious culture when sneaking off to another church is risky.

The pastor talked about love so much that the church we worked at eventually banned his book. But I had already read it, and I told everyone around the fire pit about it; they raised their eyebrows. I think they all had the same idea that my home church had: you belong to one place, not two. This was around the same time our fancy church said from the stage that no one should ever read *Harry Potter* or go to see the movie. I had already read that book too; I'd anxiously stood in line the night it came out. And Michael and I drove two hours out of town to see the movie so we wouldn't get caught by one of the congregation's ten thousand members and be put to death—"or worse, expelled!" as Hermione Granger would say.

Those nights by the fire and at the church down the road were the start of a deep questioning for me. It's the first time I felt safe enough to doubt what I had been handed, when I could finally look back at the dot I'd come from and name what had happened, name the ideology I'd formed. I was stretching out the line I was walking on ever so slightly, daring to wonder whether my tribe had it right after all. But I was also feeling my cynical heart wrestling with itself. Right when I was finding there was more room for the people I used to disregard, I was judging the people back on my dot and in the fancy church. Right when I found there was more room for science and less room for certainty, I looked down on anyone who wasn't going through the same religious awakening. I began to praise all that I could see stretching out in front of me while looking behind and judging all of the people dancing and waving their hands in freedom, thinking they were so stuck in shallow theology and feelings.

The fire grows, burning some things up and sending more sparks into the sky, and I realize I'm changing. I want to dig beneath what I have taken at face value, what I have thought is true because it's what my tribe handed me. It is here I feel safe enough to lean closer to the flames and whisper, "I have already read *Harry Potter*," and, "I don't think I am a Republican." The Christians gasp. Shannon, my wild art-school friend, cheers because she is already liberal. Jadranka the Croatian laughs hard because it's such an American confession.

Bread, Wine, and Mary Jane

We drove slowly as blankets of snow covered us. We were in the dead center of a blizzard, unable to see even ten feet ahead of us. I rolled down my window to let the flakes touch my skin—they felt like feathers—then my hand began to burn from the frigid cold, so I rolled the window up fast. It was in my early years that the Colorado mountains took root in my bones—their crisp air tinged with the smell of pine and a hint of Mary Jane. We'd dreamed for years about moving there, but we became scared, then comfortable with our job and nice house, and then brave, and so here we were, about to hit the state line, leaving Michigan.

With dreams in our heads, we drove as people with dreams do—scared and excited all at once. Scared to leave what we had come from, excited about everything ahead.

At first we were laughing and singing, and then I said something about how we could learn to snowboard tomorrow, and I burst into tears. "We don't have jobs or health insurance—we can't learn to snowboard! What if we break something and can't pay for the crazy hospital bills and end up living on the streets?"

And what were we doing moving to Colorado? Were we out of our minds? We were musicians for the love, leaving a well-paying job, good friends, our cozy firepit circle, and an interior architecture job I had just interviewed for back in Michigan. We were leaving the comfort behind not because we were so great and risky but because we had to. We both felt we had hung on too long, stayed comfortable too long, become jaded, and that wasn't good for us or anyone else.

And so that was how we found ourselves driving to Denver with nothing but a suitcase, plus an air mattress, minus health insurance and jobs. We drove as snow covered all of the life underneath it. I wondered what was dying in the ground as we drove on. I rolled my window down again and let the snow chill my skin, let the flakes fall fast.

Colorado is the linchpin of my story. And it's strange—we all make decisions, ones we think are affecting only our lives. Then later we realize that decisions and marriages and babies all came from that one drive through the snow, that one meet-up for coffee, that one hello on the steps by the payphone. It is sobering how such small things add up.

It is all vapor, really—our entire lives the tiniest blips in the ever-expanding universe. But our decisions are connected. If we had turned back that snowy night, if we hadn't said yes, I wonder how much of the rest of this story would not have happened. How much was a product of our decisions, and how much was in the cards all along?

We celebrated Christmas with a bare Christmas tree and lounged on an old sofa I bought on Craigslist. Our belongings were who knows where because the moving company never arrived and they couldn't recall ever speaking with us. So we had paper plates and disposable silverware for eating with, one pot for cooking.

We loved everything about Denver. Our thrill with life went up as our bank account went down, down. But we felt too alive to care about security. Two months in, our small section of boxes was found. A dresser and vacuum were missing but we gained a stranger's rug.

Icy chill gave way to warmer days, and we found ourselves traveling more, writing more. My feminist friend Rachael and I talked about what it means to love and found it is more profound than we'd previously thought, because no one is excluded. She is a kind-of-hippy girl who doesn't shower very much and cries in the most beautiful way I have ever seen. We met at this really big youth event that attracted ten to thirty thousand teenagers. We were the band; she was one of the actresses. She is an artist through and through, loves to be naked at the hot springs, and one day she got punched in the face at a dance club for casually misting people without their knowing, which says a lot about her playfulness and sass and also explains why I like Rachael.

She is my soul sister through and through, and she decided to move to Denver. In the future we will have years of late-night talks, Monday-morning coffee, and I'll dart to her office to deliver life-altering news. I'll be in her wedding. We will travel America together.

She will be at my side when I face the hardest day of my life. She will cry with me and we'll hug each other in the far booth at the corner coffee shop. But that will be later. For now, she moved downtown and we decided to have church in our tiny apartment. More friends joined us in the living room, and it grew. From three to thirty to "oh, wow, we need a bigger space." So we found a basement.

Candles flickered, sending light dancing on faces, and the scents of vanilla and patchouli hovered. It was Sunday night, and everyone was gathered in a circle in the basement of an old church. I looked around and wondered where all of these people came from.

Sometimes people are bound by the thread of what they are not; they are bound by the dot they left behind or a sort of enemy that gives them all something to rally against. We all left something rigid and structured in search of something intimate, something we probably labeled, "More real, just, organic, ya know?" It was the era when *organic* was used all the time, improperly more than properly. But gradually we all began looking at the line stretched out in front of us and decided what we were for instead of what we were against. It became a brave new world where people of faith could do things like swear, drink wine, and come out of the closet. It was a place for everyone to belong.

We bought a very official, very actual sign after much debate about whether there should be a sign at all. Suddenly it was a regular thing that people called their home, bound by inclusion, love, vulnerability, and hipster clothes. Michael and I found ourselves flying across the country to play a show with our band, then flying back to set up chairs, play more music, talk a bit, then fold all the chairs back up, clean the floor and restroom, and make a lost-and-found box.

We believed in the way of Jesus, that it is good and true, but we didn't believe we'd cornered the market on truth, because we'd begun ripping up that idea in Michigan. Still, with a lot of ego, Michael and I had left the big fancy church thinking that our new way of "doing church" was so much better and true—no fancy things, no passing the offering for people's money, no altar calls, no one guy ruling the show, no judgments. We attracted seventeen- to twenty-three-year-olds like moths to a flame, repelled older folks like pepper spray.

Maybe it was us? Maybe it was because we met in a basement?

Maybe it was the rat that did it. This guy Cody always showed up with a rat on his shoulder. Sometimes Cody would play in the band, and sure enough, there the rat would be. Cody loved the rat, and we weren't quite sure how to tell him it kind of freaked all of us out. But we wanted to be open, to have the weird and marginalized people feel more welcome than anyone, and apparently it worked.

We dug into the community to find ways to support people. We helped build beds, gave food, created a relationship with the children and staff at an orphanage in Kenya. We mentored at-risk kids in Denver, had potlucks and park days. We baptized people in the lake, handed out water and watermelon at shelters on hot summer days, and sang for hours on end until we were once again folding up chairs, cleaning up the floor, filling up the lost-and-found box.

After a while, we were exhausted and in desperate need of help. After some good old-fashioned schmoozing and begging, Michael's lifelong friend from Oklahoma finally said yes to taking over as pastor. He was supported by a church that, amazingly, believed in our little raggedy group. It just so happened that it was Michael's father's church. I think Michael's father was biased. We hired our friend Jamie, found a rhythm, and suddenly, we were a well-organized group of not only eighteen-year-olds but also real live families: the Barrets, the Mertens, Doorman, Stamps, Waller, Harvey, Purdy, Chuck Wilson with the fine mustache, Amie and Amy and Aimee, Bultman, Hornsbee, Bean, the Arndts—the list went on with kids and adults that all made up what we felt was the best of tribes. We slowly went from thirty to four hundred, plus one rat.

And so the line was rich with inclusion, open discussion about beliefs, and a lot of chaos, and more than anything, it was a place to belong. We began as two kids with grand egos out to change the world, but the flesh and blood that embodied that world began doing something to us we didn't expect. It unearthed more heart, more empathy, which brought greater perspective to see people as they are. It began to unearth beliefs we never knew were poisonous, and it will be the place that unearths every belief I have.

Neighbors and Lady Tubes

The first house we bought in Denver came with cocaine-dealing neighbors and weekly gunshots. My parents were less than thrilled with our purchase, as were Michael's parents. As was most anyone else. Their concern arose in seeing all of the dilapidated houses looking as if they would fall over with the slightest breeze, then escalated when the inebriated came banging on our door at 4:00 a.m. Our neighbors informed us that only a decade ago, they slept on the floor so middle-of-the-night gunfire wouldn't accidentally come through the windows and kill them. I shouldn't have told my parents this.

But I loved our neighborhood and our tiny house with the white-trimmed circle window in the kitchen. It all felt so human—old and new, paint covering cracks, rich and aged. We wanted to be in the center of Denver life, and for us, that meant living on the edge of downtown, right next to its people.

And so this is how I met Paul, our neighbor, who became our dear friend of eight years, who taught me what it means to be selfless, and how forgiveness should be on repeat, how to cherish a thirty-year-old single-malt whiskey on the front porch.

John and Paul had been married for fifteen years. They were two gruff, gray-haired tough guys with tatted-up arms and were as sweet as they come. Before we moved in, I was standing on the sidewalk admiring our purchase when Paul said, "Ah, I think it just sold!" Before I could say hello, he added with sarcasm and a laugh, "I think it sold to some young weird Christian band!" I said, "Oh, um . . . yeah, well, that's us." We stared at each other, then he roared with laughter. He couldn't believe two scrawny Christian kids were moving into this neighborhood.

"You know this is a gay neighborhood, right?"

"Er . . . no, I didn't. But I'm okay with that."

Again, he belly laughed, and we were instant friends. I knew my parents wouldn't approve of our house or our neighbors.

John and Paul brought over bread and wine and we cele-brated our new home in the middle of moving boxes. I could call when I needed help with absolutely anything, use their endless variety of power tools, ask them to come over in the middle of the night when I was scared because Michael was out of town.

Paul heard a song of ours that says, "God is Love, God is Love, and he loves everyone—atheists and charlatans and com-munists and lesbians."

Paul looked at me blankly and said, "But I thought God hated gay people."

Though he tried to play it off, the pain was clear in his eyes. There were days stories would unravel of heartache and the struggle to accept himself. He had been rejected, faced our harsh society and enough religious rants for a lifetime. I thought about all of the rants I had said out loud and in my head years back.

We continued to have parties, handed wine over our red brick wall, handed over rakes and eggs, and at the end of a long day, we'd sit on the front porch until the early hours, doing the small talk that leads to deep conversations. The scary-close conversations where secrets you hide come brimming to the surface, afraid to be seen but just needing someone else to tell you, "I get it. I've been there."

I thought about where I had come from, the tribe I was in and the ideas they had about Paul's life. How I was told who was in and who was out, and how that idea had changed dramatically.

We heard more stories in the basement and on the front porch—of shame and people wrestling with their religion, sexuality, existence. And I used to have an answer for the story even though a question wasn't asked. It's in this beautiful line that I found my labels for people failing. My way of thinking was challenged by every story I heard, every stone of dogma upturned. Denver became the place I dug my hands into earth and saw how it wasn't so much that I was cultivating it as it was cultivating me. And I thought I had so much wisdom to hand out. Each Sunday night that we gathered, and every time I headed over to Paul's porch at the end of the day, I found truth was more a thing my tribe didn't own. I found that love was much bigger than my idea of it.

I did not discover this on stages; I discovered it in basements and on front porches.

Four years in Michigan not trying.

Two years in Michigan not preventing.

Four years in Denver trying, trying, trying.

"Hi, my name is Lisa, and I can't get pregnant."

It felt like this was plastered to my forehead. It became my badge, my scarlet letter.

I looked at the pee stick and threw it in the trash. Negative, again. I changed my diet, planned it all out—with my cycle, the moon, the planets. I got acupuncture. I saw a fertility specialist, had blood drawn, endured a thing-a-ma-bob in the baby maker, got dye injected into my lady tubes, put my legs in the air for fifteen minutes. But still, no baby in said maker.

Michael and I decide to take the adoption path. I knew it would be years before a baby or child was in our arms. So I braced myself for years.

Then amazingly, my sister knew a girl. She was sixteen, pregnant and afraid, and she was considering terminating. I braced myself. We jumped on the phone, told her we would love to adopt her baby if she would carry it. She said yes. I couldn't believe it.

It was fate. It happened so fast. It was over in six months.

It's a good story, really. She grew attached to her baby once she was able to feel it kick. She bonded. Her whole family surrounded her and decided to help out. I knew it was a good thing, but on an airplane going home from a tour, I cried happy tears for the baby and the mother and also sad tears for myself. I downed three glasses of wine because there were no children for me? I would be a wine connoisseur and drink to my heart's content while all of my lame pregnant friends made wonderful bundles of joy and ruined their party lives.

I sat in the middle of a friend's living room and cried, felt my heart wrestle with itself. We kept traveling and singing. We saw Rome and Paris. We sang. We visited Poland and Uganda. We saw poverty and oppression like we hadn't seen before, saw evil that was hard to absorb. I dropped onto the chair at the piano and tried to process.

Where are you, God? You saw this? I thought you were good. I thought you were listening. I thought you were . . . over and over again. *How can I pray for a child? I looked at all of the children's shoes in that room in Auschwitz, all of the hair and suitcases. I walked the same ground they did on the way to the crematoriums, went inside the haunted gas chamber that took their sacred lives. I'm sure they prayed too. I'm sure they begged. Did you hear the sound? So how can I ask for a baby, let alone anything, now that I have seen this?*

I felt my eyes opening to my deeply rooted Western mindset, my privilege. The lens I saw the world through cracked and splintered, the line I was walking on now shaking with uncertainty about a good God who loves his children.

I once heard a man say he had favor on his life because he received a good parking spot at the mall. I cringed. I'd thought something like that before, believed it—like it was a blessing having a nice house or car or having something come easily. How did I ever believe that? The great American dream bastardizing the profound story of Love. I realized how often I had abducted the story, how I'd labeled certain things as favor, blessing, transaction. I wondered what the kids I knew in Kenya or the people in Auschwitz called favor. A bread crumb? Death?

God and I weren't seeing eye to eye. If this were my world, it would be better than this violent dog-eat-dog one here. This one isn't fair. It doesn't hand out what is deserved in proper portions. There is too much pain, too much poverty and present hell. How are we to swallow it and not be poisoned? And how am I to swallow the idea that there is a God asking us to just hold on until we die and are freed of this world he created? We just had to keep bailing water out of the boat until the afterlife, but I wanted to jump ship now.

I went to the piano, fidgeted with its ivory keys, then played. I let music wrap me up like it had since I sat in that overstuffed orange rocking chair and those trees in my front yard. I let music do what it has always done—untie, connect, breathe.

I thought about our bodies being made of things like dust and water and swirling atoms of ordered chaos. I thought about life feeling like a pile of swirling dirt and chaos—no order. I thought about all of the people who faced something hard and what they did with it. They often spoke of something beautiful coming from the broken places. I began singing a melody, then sang words: "You make beautiful things out of the dust." I sang it over and over, then abandoned it because no, things were not becoming more beautiful; it was all entropy.

There was a surgery, more hope, then again nothing. I didn't want to stick another needle in my skin or hope our child was already alive. One day while sitting in my car, I pulled over by the trees and called Michael, told him I was giving up. He prayed for us; I couldn't. I held the phone to my ear with one hand and looked at my other hand clenched tight in my lap. His prayer was more a prayer of letting go than asking for something, reposturing our hearts to know that anything we had or didn't have was never ours anyway. I remembered the trees outside and the feeling of gaining a small breath. I opened my hands to the plain truth we would never have biological children.

It was a hard emotional turn, one of those sharp lefts in life. Especially when faith was centered so much on believing things into existence. I wasn't sure what I believed about God doing things or not doing things, but I felt the suffering I had been carrying around like a badge ceased, all because I opened my hands to what was, opened my eyes to what was.

So instead of kids, Michael and I would raise dogs, I thought, maybe birds, definitely not cats. Maybe we could try adoption again down the road, but for now I'd keep being a rad aunt. And have perky boobs—I'd keep that too.

I went back to the piano, sang, "You make beautiful things," and felt I believed it. Not because something was gained but because something was let go, which felt like a truer gain—an unattachment to what I thought I needed.

A Teacher

People often ask where the turning point was for us in music. It was once we stopped scraping and trying to get someone, anyone to like our music, once we began creating unafraid of what vulnerability might cost us. We became more honest with the wrestle of life. Once we stopped caring what honesty might mean for our acceptance, that's when our career changed.

My mother called and said, "I heard your song on the radio!"

We started receiving letters, emails, downloads. The song that held so much struggle for us hit something deep in others as well, and people began singing it all over the world. I was stunned. The feeling of pain wrecking us and hoping that something good would come of heartbreak—this is universal.

Suddenly things moved fast—tours, interviews, recording. We traded neighborhood and home life for a minivan, then for a twelve-bunk bus. The band became family. We slept in late (around noon), found coffee (fair trade and organic, please), set up and sound checked (always painfully long), then played music and partied on the bus after. We believed in each other and in the art, and we felt deep in our bones this is what we were made for—to open the human heart through music.

We got tired, wanted our own beds, became irritated when

someone left toothpaste spit in the sink of the one-square-inch bathroom or left Chinese food in the fridge (Michael). Once, our guitar player got so sick of this massive bowl of puppy mix our cellist's mother gave her that he marched out of the bus and drop kicked it, sending Chex mix and powdered sugar flying. And way more than once we had dance parties with strobe lights flashing on our phones. Bus life is an interesting life. And the shows felt like magic—all of us together, the crowd, the band, all as one. I would stare out at the crowds, at my bandmates, and think, *I can't believe I get to experience this. I can't believe this is my life.*

We traveled the States, Europe, Asia, Canada, did big shows and small ones, arena shows and house shows. Once, we played a show with our instrument cables running through the windows of a house and plugged into a 120 amp outlet. It was no surprise when the power shut off. Another show, Michael fell through the stage, but he kept playing, didn't miss a beat. Me, I couldn't regain my composure after seeing him play his guitar while standing up to his waist in a hole.

Some shows had tens of thousands; some had not so much. We played our hearts out and toured the world. I felt like the small-town nobody who somehow got lucky. All of the times I sat with my brother at the piano singing, all of the hours I spent in the chili fields and in the late-night "holy roller" services, I never thought I would make a dime on a song, let alone have a music career. After all of the years of feeling I didn't really belong, I felt I had found my place in the world. Here I was, right beside the love of my life. two creative people making a living in music—the luck of that didn't escape either of us. We made up songs everywhere—in the car, lying in bed, walking down the street, in locker rooms and crappy hotels. I loved all of it.

Denver got cold, then warm, then cold again as a year passed. Somewhere in between doing a show and getting on an airplane, we landed in urgent care. Michael had choked on a Philly cheese steak and tore his esophagus. I had never heard of such a thing and thought he would surely die as I saw him sputtering and barfing up bits of blood. He sat on the paper-covered patient bed, and I remembered I was late on getting some shots after a trip to Africa. Before I could receive the shots, the doctor had to be certain I wasn't knocked up. He pricked my finger and left for ten minutes. Michael and I laughed, realizing that at one point my heart would have been in my throat while taking such a test, hoping, crossing my fingers.

"Good thing I don't expect that anymore!" I said and rolled my eyes. Michael half laughed with his torn esophagus.

The doctor came back into the room, looking at a clipboard.

"Well, according to the calendar, it looks as though we are looking around the beginning or middle of . . . looks like August."

I looked down at his notes, a scribble of numbers.

"What?" I asked. The scribble wasn't legible in the least.

"I mean, we can't be sure when, but if you can't remember when you had your last period . . . maybe August?" he responded.

"I don't know what you are saying to me."

"Um . . . well, er . . . you are due in August. You are pregnant. Isn't that why you're here?" He pointed to a plus sign in his notes.

I stared open mouthed at Michael and screamed. I was out of body, really out of urgent care entirely. My tears were instant, and I wasn't sure I was breathing. Just yells, all yelling and laughing and clapping. We must have been a sight—me jumping and screaming, Michael in pain but jumping and hugging me and laughing. The doctor was wide eyed. "This is the best reaction I have ever seen!" he said, and he belly laughed.

We hugged the doctor like he was my fairy godfather, at last making a baby magically appear in my uterus.

I couldn't say it fast enough after we rushed home and called her first. "Mom! I'm pregnant!" She lost herself in tears and laughing.

We called family. I raced to Rachael's work, and we danced in the stairwell. Bre and Jamie danced around their tiny apartment and took a picture of my pre-protruding belly. We announced it at our church and everyone cheered. I barely held it together the first time we sang "Beautiful Things" at a show, knowing a little baby was growing a heart, lungs, a little body right at that moment.

And I am glad for this—this baby was not the final blessing after a bout of suffering. I didn't see her as the grand revelation of some guy in the sky telling me I had finally learned and now had favor. Learning unattachment was a gift, and the baby, another.

The day she comes into our lives:

I labor with pain and a little bit of fear because it is my first time. My mother and mother-in-law (Momma G) sit with their ears pressed to the door, whispering and laughing. Our gang of friends sleeps in the waiting room, and with each contraction, I think surely my life will end.

But I focus, turn inward and center in a way I have never experienced. It is during pregnancy and labor that I realize the power of a woman's body—how it has been thinking, creating, healing without my realizing it, and now I see it fully. My body has been doing this thing, this miraculous human-growing thing that I do not consciously make happen or think into being. It's just doing it all on its own—intelligent body.

Right as I think I can't push anymore or hear the words "pelvic floor" ever again, she makes her entrance into the world and takes a breath.

She is put on my body, right up on my chest—the world and everything in it stops. She is perfect. Pure magic.

Michael and I smile at each other with expressions that say "are you seeing this?" It is astounding to make an actual human with someone, to create tiny eyelashes and toes, eyes that look right up at you. The emotion of it takes all our words away, leaves us only watching and feeling completely new things.

Then Michael timidly asks if her cone-shaped head will morph into a less cone-shaped head or if it will be like that forever, and the nurses laugh. We've waited so long for this girl. Love takes on entirely new depths.

She will continue to rearrange our hearts and our sleeping schedule the next four years. She will become the bus baby, the sweetheart of the entire band. She will wake us all up in the middle of the night; she will make us all laugh as she learns to talk and her aunt Lissa teaches her all the bad words. She will play hide and seek in the bunks; she will dance on stage and blow me kisses from the back curtain, then always fall asleep as we start the show. Our music will be her sleep cue.

I will hold my arms out to her as she learns to walk on a cobblestone street in Belgium. We will see the remains of castles in Ireland and hurried street cars in London. We will all get drenched at Niagara Falls and lie in the sun in California. I will hold her as calls of congratulations come in after we receive Grammy nominations. I will hold her in the recording booth and laugh at how unbelievable our life is becoming. It will all feel so unreal. Michael, she, and I will be the three musketeers, and we will take on the world together.

But right after her birth, she lies on me and I just stare. I am undone. I am thoroughly convinced no one has ever loved their child more than I love her.

And here my sturdy line begins to shake again. How can it? This is the miracle child. Shouldn't this make everything more solid? But my ideas on love, eternity, truth—the lines I have been teetering on the edge of—they disappear in the wake of experiencing mother love. Seeing this girl makes everything expand. There is no limit to my love for her, nothing she can possibly do to lose it. I see her body and think it is perfect, born from love, so how can she ever escape my love or cause me to turn my face from her? And so my construct of God and faith again expand in the wake of this new perspective.

We never know how the credits will roll, who will fill what part, who will find the truth or miss it entirely. The moment she comes into my arms, she changes everything.

What I don't know is that in four years, she will give the hospital halls color. She will play doctor while I wait with knots in my chest. She will be the one to see the wires and worried faces but see past all of it.

She will be the one to see the truth so many of us will miss.

Bottom of the Cup

The great religions are the ships, poets the lifeboats. Every sane person I know has jumped overboard.

—HAFEZ

We walked miles at night, up and down Cherry Street as we pushed Amelie in the red stroller. I can still see the way my shoes looked, feel the way my brow furrowed. His statement hung in the air, unflinching.

In earlier months we walked because it helped fuel new ideas and budding dreams. Sometimes our conversation was thick with debate about beliefs. Sometimes we talked about the kids we were both mentoring, how one believed he was a vampire and the other believed she wasn't worth much at all. Or about how weird it was that we were actual parents.

Sometimes we were silent in thought, wrestling.

But let's say our faith was like a sweater. Yarn: our ideology. Weave: our tradition. This is how you wear it. Don't change it, even if the sweater doesn't keep you warm anymore. Even if it's too tight or the threads cut off oxygen at your neck. This is the way. Doubts and questions mean disrespect, and those are the seeds of evil, so just don't.

But over the years, a thread comes loose and you try to just tuck it in alongside the others. You can cover the fraying up. You can pull the thread and think, *Oh, I don't need this one, because it is harmful to me; it's itchy and gets caught on corners.* It comes out easily. And the sweater stays together. Then you pull another, and another, and soon you find all the yarn is gone. You have deconstructed the entire thing. You are left naked. People gawk and run away, and you feel two opposing things: the freedom of glorious nakedness, and the fear of the same.

I'd thought this night would be like the others. I paused to tuck a blanket around Amelie's feet as we pulled at metaphorical strings, figuring out which threads to weave back together and which to set on fire. Michael jumped into a thought I can't quite remember.

What I do remember is this: "I don't think I believe in God anymore."

Did I hear Michael right? Yeah, we questioned, ripped apart our theology to see what truth could stand the fight, but he doesn't believe anymore at all? My husband is telling me he's an atheist?

Fear crawled up my back like a wild animal. My thoughts were frenzied. Sure, I had questions. I had shocked Michael through the years with my own "hypocrisy" at times. But this conversation was different. He didn't just have questions about God but had come to the conclusion that there is not one.

I felt tricked. Some person had invaded my husband, changing brain wires around, deceiving him. What about all of our history? We had even started a church together, still had a church to lead. I wanted to call someone, run to someone who would understand and have advice. But who could I run to with this? We were the ones people came to with questions. We were supposed to be the leaders, the answer holders.

I didn't think I could go to family because I knew what the argument would be. I knew all of the answers they would give, and how exactly do you look at your parents and tell them Bible answers don't work because it's so hard to believe the Bible? I hadn't told them it was about seven months since I had last read the Scriptures they so esteemed, that there were things throughout them that made me deeply sad, angry, and confused each time I read them. So many people told me it was simple, and I wondered why I couldn't see it that way. I could read Proverbs, and Song of Solomon with all of its sexy talk, but that was about it. Michael asked me not to tell anyone about this because for many people the Bible is above Jesus himself. But now Michael decided to take a giant leap forward to nonbelief? Great. My Bible issues were gravy.

So I'd have to have that conversation first, then tell them my husband had abandoned the family religion. Anyone any-where knew it was going to be a terrible conversation, a tribal war. I might as well have told them my husband was a terrorist. Avoidance sounded way, way better.

We had already stretched our religion to the max, given up on any of the ideology of "us against them" or "guy in the sky." We had already been the black sheep, but now we were . . . what? The dead sheep?

I couldn't tell my best friend, Rachael; I didn't want to scare her. I couldn't tell Bre or Jamie; I didn't want to freak them out or give them any unrequested doubts of their own. I didn't think there was anyone I could hand this kind of bomb to.

I mean, this was us. Michael sang about God every day, even on our wedding day, when the half-alive butterfly flew up into the heavens.

This wasn't what I'd signed up for. This wasn't us. I'd signed up with the guy who was on the same page as me, the guy who was undoing and knitting back together the same faith as me, not throwing it all away. He'd pulled me out of downward spirals. He'd helped me see the light. If his foundation had changed, who would he become?

And it hit me. Would we last?

Ten years of marriage, and I had never had that thought before. It was never on the table. He was it for me, my soul mate. We always said we would die lying next to each other in our sleep at 120 years old, or we'd die right after sex at 120 years old. But that was always with the idea that we would die believing we'd meet up in heavenly bliss, not eternal nothingness.

So I pushed the stroller and stayed silent.

The Scripture "do not be unequally yoked" loomed above my head.

I thought about all of the stories I had heard of people who just couldn't make it work, as hard as they tried. I thought about my parents—they subscribed to the same religion, different denominations. And it still didn't work.

So how would this work? How would we stay connected yet believe different things? Because I did believe in God. I just didn't believe like most of the other Christians. And how in the world could we raise a family together? What would this mean for our church and our career and the rest of my life?

I knew the world we both grew up in—either you are in or you are out, "us, the truth holders" or "them, the blinded." Michael was now an outsider, and maybe, really, I was too, because I was this weird, what, half believer? I knew the tribe we were in; I knew what they said about people like us. I knew what they said about atheists like him.

When I was a kid, my dad walked into the kitchen one day and bet me he could lose more than eight pounds via a quick trip to the restroom. My siblings and I were appalled. I said there was no way possible and accepted the bet. A bit later, with a smirk and a strut, he announced he had lost eight pounds. *Eight pounds*. He, the winner, and I, ten dollars poorer.

About fifteen years later, I recounted this story to some friends while my dad was present, and we laughed hysterically at the absurdity and utter repugnancy of his feat. I looked at him, eager to see embarrassment flood his face, but he was not red faced like I thought he should be. He just looked at me with a smirk.

"It was pennies," he said.

I stopped laughing.

"What?"

"I loaded up my coat pockets with pennies, then I went into the restroom and took them out."

I was stunned. I couldn't believe it. "No . . . no, you went to the restroom . . . and . . ."

"Just pennies." He exploded in laughter. "I can't believe you didn't know after all this time!"

The story I had carried around for fifteen years was not

the amazing, ridiculous, gross, unbelievable story I thought it to be. It was false. And it's silly—knowing how sly my dad was, I should have known all along. My inner self bowed its head in embarrassment at my belief. I should have known better.

But I think we all feel this. We believe, then feel tricked at some point. We believe magic is everywhere because it is everywhere—the soil, the stars, the bugs we dig up in the dirt, and winged things we see in the sky. But then it all begins to feel so normal because we see it every day and busy our lives with looking for other magical things like cancer miraculously disappearing. Our hearts break or someone fails us and the magic gets sucked out.

Maybe for you it was the other way around. Maybe explaining the science of the world made your heart come alive, explaining how tribalism can blind us freed you swiftly and easily. Not me. Because I was given concrete answers to how the world was made and was told questioning it was a sin. I was told how our sacred texts were to be interpreted, who was in and who was out, what is sinful to do and what isn't, answers to it all, and when I discovered those answers were not certain, I felt tricked by the people I'd trusted, and tricked by my naive self; another pocketful of pennies discovered.

When I was on the dot, it felt like I was part of this grand resistance, fighting against an evil system, winning all the lost. And I felt this way on the line too. But the more we traveled and saw behind the curtain of beliefs, the more I saw doctrine and rules overpowering love. I saw people living one way in public and another in private, the powerful silencing the weak. I read news articles of priests hurting thousands of children, the rebels becoming the oppressors. And I began to see how truth didn't belong to one tribe. I saw control unfold in the name of God. It was like I thought I was part of the resistance but slowly realized I was part of the empire.

My cynicism, skepticism, and doubt grew, and I wouldn't be tricked again. I believed in God, but I was losing faith in the Christian or any organized religion. I wondered if there were more tricks, and I felt tricked by Michael. This wasn't who he told me he would be.

We continued walking after I listened to Michael's confession. I realized I hadn't looked up even once. We just walked as I pushed Amelie's stroller. I looked right at him. He looked like the same person. I supposed I anticipated horns or a tail sprouting, but he just looked the same. A different thought came: I loved him. And he had loved me through all of my doubts and beliefs. He had let me say my worst fears because he knew I needed to have a safe place. If I didn't let him be honest with me, if I rejected him now, what would rejection do to him?

What was this love I touted and believed if it wasn't holding him close even in this? I saw countless couples not able to be honest with each other, and consequently, they found someone else they could be honest with. My expectation that he would believe no matter what and be a heroic knight in shining armor that everyone esteems was too high, irrational. I said I wanted vulnerability, but really, did I? Because in that moment, I didn't want to hear about shadows and uncertainty. I wanted his wrestling with belief to make belief stronger, not kill God.

But though we weren't precisely on the same page, I knew how he came to this conclusion—disappointment; moral failures

of so many spiritual leaders, including his father; belief contra-
dicting science; the fact that some people get big houses and some
people are slaves; and then there are children who are forced to
do things, unspeakable things. It's the problem of pain, and if you
ever really think about it, it will be at least perplexing and at most
cause you to believe there is no loving God at all.

We were supposed to lead music at our church in two days.
Michael was supposed to speak. This nonbelief put a bit of a
twist on leading a whole group of people who gather around
faith. He asked if he should tell people where he was, and we
both knew the answer to that question. We had agreed long ago
that we would be open and honest. This was our community,
our family. We couldn't hide the questions we were wrestling
with. He couldn't get up and say one thing but believe another.
"I think you should be honest," I said.

We walked into the little basement once again. Candles
flickered once again. People gathered in a circle and we sang
together, then Michael stood up. He explained his struggle, how
it had come to this, and how he was trying to keep his heart
open. He said, "I don't know that I can believe anything right
now." I went between feeling like I was going to throw up and
feeling like I going to laugh hysterically: "This is funny, right?
Your pastor doesn't believe in God! Bwahahaha! *Right?*"

"But I'm here, and I'm open," he said. He went with other
things but I can't remember because I was biting all of my nails
off and planning my exit route. We ended the night with a song
and stuck around a while to talk with people—exit route failed.

The first person came up. "Thank you for being honest."
The next: "I feel the same way." Our eyes widened. Another
person: "I have the same questions. I'll see you next Sunday."

There was one woman who was livid. "How do you expect to pastor a church when you don't even know what you believe?" Good point. She left and said she would never come back.

Another person walked up, hugged me, and said, "That must have been hard for him to share. Thank you for being honest. See you soon."

We were shocked. We felt embraced.

"Um . . . that went well," I said, and we looked at each other with curiosity, like we somehow missed the mob.

It felt strange driving home. We were prepared for life to collapse, but instead we grabbed food with our regular gang like it was any regular Sunday. But confessing to people and walking it out proved to be two different things, the way a thirty-minute speech is always different from the practicalities of life. In a week I found myself staring at the wood floor in the bathroom, scared we were falling off the face of the earth. I held my head in my hands. It hurt. I kept waiting for something to change in Michael. Now that his confession was out, wasn't a cloud supposed to appear or a donkey speak? We didn't have a donkey, but I assumed our dog would work, considering. I felt betrayed by God. It felt like I had let go of the idols containing who or what God is, but if there was a God, wouldn't he/she/it be kind enough to show someone who was begging to see? I played the piano, stayed silent within the forest, did all of the usual things to open my heart to hear. I tried to be the strong wife, unwavering, even though it felt like I was bailing water out of a sinking boat. I had this terrible feeling Michael was right and there was no God; maybe I was just too scared to say it.

When you have lived your entire life certain there is some great God in the process of saving everything, and when your entire life is framed around that notion, the loss of it is a deep grief. I felt like I was losing two things—God and my soul mate. Michael and I just couldn't talk about God like we used to. *I* couldn't even talk about God like I used to to anyone else. It's like the language didn't work anymore. The words I had always used had been used too much and were so packed with assumptions they caused a negative reaction in me. Writing songs together was hard. We just didn't know what to say because we saw the world as different colors. I missed our spur-of-the-moment songs, our little practice room where we sang for hours. I missed the security of certainty.

So I began ignoring the conversation, shutting that part of me down because it just hurt too much. I thought maybe I could just wait it out and eventually I'd feel better.

Shutting the conversation down helped me have good days. We would play with Amelie, and our hearts exploded with love for her. We'd hike in the mountains and enjoy long dinners with friends in our back yard.

On the hard days I cried on the floor in the bathroom, pleading to God to do something. Even just to help us raise a child and not screw her up because one parent says there is no God and the other prays with her in secret at night, then feels guilty. Because as I held her little hands to pray, there was a taunting voice in my head saying, "You don't even believe what you are saying. How can you pray for your child to be safe when other parents have prayed the same and they were not safe? How can you pray for Michael to change when underneath it all you are angry that God doesn't stop genocide and war and famine? How dare you pray; it doesn't do anything." What if the belief I was handing my daughter was so full of holes it would one day lead my daughter and me to fight until we were exhausted—like my mother and I were beginning to do. Talking about faith used to be this exciting thing, this beautiful tether between my mother and me. And now what would I say?

I wondered what my mother thought. Secrets spread through the family, and I could only imagine how it sounded. Me, the good girl once on the "straight and narrow," with Grammy-nominated songs and singing about God all over the world, now blinded by evil, or her evil husband, and forever to burn in the eternal pit of despair because I was doubting.

I didn't know how to broach the subject with her, just how to explain each doubt and why it was there. I knew what her answers would be; I used to use those same answers. "Just trust and believe!" And I didn't know how to explain the freedom and fear that came with this doubt, feeling scared but also enlivened by new ideas. Shame and fear pulled me back. Wonder pulled me forward. I didn't have the language for what was happening, and so I couldn't really explain what was happening. It felt like I was wandering without a destination or even a roadmap, and that is a tough feeling when all your life you've had a single direction.

Lousy Atheist

**We are all atheists about most of the
gods that humanity has ever believed in.
Some of us just go one god further.**

—Richard Dawkins

Edamame." I let the word roll off my tongue. We were in Denver, sitting at our favorite ramen spot in the Highlands.

"I think people like saying this word," I said. "I like saying it because it makes me feel interesting and cultured."

Michael rolled his eyes.

I drummed my fingers while we waited for our ramen bowls outside in the sunlight. I let out a breath.

"What's up?" Michael asked.

"I just . . . I just feel like my heart is being tortured," I said.

"Why?"

It had been about six months since Michael's confession on Cherry Street. He was a bit on the outskirts of atheism, if there is such a thing, dipping his toes into mysticism. I had thought I was dancing in mysticism myself, but then found I'd crashed. Which points to how deeply belief can be rooted in our bones.

Mixed with all of the aforementioned reasons to doubt, I learned a cousin of mine had cancer. A kidney transplant years ago was going sour; he needed a new one to save his life. But he couldn't get one because he had cancer. His body was always battling something. He was always so close to his deathbed—kidney failing, cancer killing.

A week previously we had received news that he was miraculously healed.

I couldn't believe it. I got the call from a family member one beautiful day while staring out at the lake.

"The tumors . . . they are gone!"

"Really?" I said.

"Really!" they said.

"Whoa, no way, *really?*" I said.

"Really really really!" they exclaimed and laughed-cried.

I had this rising excitement and tension all at once. I felt like the worst person in the world because I was excited but wanted to see the actual tests. That made me kick myself. I thought about all of the stories in the Bible of the doubters who just needed to have proof. Why couldn't I just believe? I'd spent years doing just that, believing until it hurt even to ask. I had heard about all of the miracles; I just was never in the right place at the right time, and that seemed pretty unfair because I felt like I believed more than anyone ever. But everyone sounded so excited right now, everyone crying and praising God, and there I was, the doubter bringing the party down. I didn't let on, but I hated how I felt.

Suddenly I missed that feeling of lifting my hands high and

praising something up in the sky for a blessing. This miracle was bringing my entire family together, so many people I never imagined saying, "Praise God! God is good!"

"God is good." How could there actually be a guy in the sky who healed my cousin but didn't heal my friend with MS in first grade? Or what about the families burned up in Nazi crematoria? I felt the torment begin again, the awful gut-wrenching spiral that I just couldn't make heads or tails of.

Everyone loved this cousin. He is just about as wonderful as a person can get. It felt like a betrayal not joining in the party.

So I decided to believe it all again. Just like that. Thought, *Well, blind faith, right? I can do it again. I can do it. I can jump back to my old belief and just forget what I have seen.* And I jumped back to the dot, the old belief I started from where there was a guy in the sky giving gifts if we just believed.

It felt wonderful at first, like returning home after a really long time. I excitedly called my family back, ready to party, ready to return "home."

The voice on the other end said, "Well, I spoke with his mother, and it looks like it was a partial healing. But isn't it great?"

"A what?" I asked.

"Well, the tumors didn't go away. They shrank a lot, about half the size now."

"But . . . they are still there? And he still has to have surgery?"

"Yeah, but . . . they shrank a little! It's a partial miracle!" they said in celebration.

I was silent. Angry. I didn't have the stomach to say what I really wanted to say. What I wanted to say was along the lines of "Partial healing? What the hell does that even mean? Are you kidding me? That's like a bad joke! It's like holding a loaf of bread over a starving person's hands but letting only a few crumbs fall. It's like a father who abandoned his child as a baby, then came home, hugged them hard, and said, 'That was nice. See ya later!' and walked out again.

"Why would you trick me into celebrating a man's healing if he's still sick, still has to have surgery, and still might die? What kind of God does that? Why would you believe in such a monster?"

That's what I wanted to say.

Instead, I said, "I'm so glad . . . yeah, it's a-ma-zing . . . me too, I love you too, bye."

This is the conversation I had two days before I found myself sitting here at a hipster ramen restaurant in Denver. And this is what I ranted about as we waited for noodles and edamame.

"I tried, I tried to just go back, and look what happened," I said.

"Why did you try?" Michael asked.

"I just, it all seemed so wonderful. And I do believe amazing things happen to our bodies that we can't explain. I just really really wanted to try again, wondered if maybe all of the other times something was wrong with me, and now, well, maybe now things are different or maybe I'm different. I wondered if I let go of some things that needed to die, maybe that's what needed to happen before my belief would work."

"You know you are torturing yourself, right?"

"Yeah. I just suddenly missed that feeling. I'm tired of being the black sheep of the family. I used to be the good one with parents proud. And now I hear about conversations with family, about how I've really disappointed everyone. And you know what they probably say, right?"

"What?" he asked.

"They probably say it's all your fault! You're the wolf in sheep's clothing! Or worse, the Antichrist!"

We laughed hard, more out of the need for comic relief.

"Yeah, they probably say that. But they don't know it was you who stopped reading the Bible first," he proclaimed with a smirk.

"Yeah, well, you stopped believing in God first."

We could keep this going for a while.

"I used to 'know that I know that I know.' Now I believe one day, then don't the next. It feels like something is wrong with me," I said.

"Maybe you should just open your hands and try not believing anything. What are you afraid will happen?"

"That's ridiculous," I said. "I'll always believe there is something I can't see, something . . . I don't know, else."

"Yeah, but what if you didn't? Does that scare you?"

"Well, yeah."

"So if fear is the only thing making you hold on, then maybe you should let go of that and see what happens. Fear is no reason to believe."

"I certainly don't believe in the God who sends his children to scream in the fires of hell just because they weren't lucky enough to be born to Christians or become Christian before they got laid out flat by a bus."

"But sometimes it feels like I already don't believe in this story. It feels like my brain has split right in two and I'm at war with myself. I don't understand why I just can't always believe. It feels like I've seen too much."

It is painful having belief unhinged. I thought I could tinker a bit with the electrical cords to make it all work better, but I suddenly found the entire house had burned to the ground.

It makes me wonder about when Jesus talks about the narrow road. This one here feels pretty narrow, this questioning whether I really have it right. Aren't questions what drives humanity forward? Imagine no one ever doubted that the earth was flat or thought that women might, in fact, be smart enough to vote. Imagine slavery was never questioned. Doubt pushes open the door to change, which opens the door to equality, justice, love, truth. I knew if we never questioned how we did things, we would stagnate, become dead people walking.

I looked at Michael. I imagined an atheist looking sadder than he did. When I was younger, atheists had been painted as the awful people who hated all of the beauty in the world and tried to bring down anyone who loved butterflies or rainbows. But Michael looked happy. Free even. These days there was no torment or angsty circles in his head, only in mine. I didn't think I had anything to lose, and I also thought God would understand and forgive me if I was wrong.

"Okay, I am an atheist," I said firmly.

I had decided. I was firm. But then a couple hours in, I was not firm. Then the very next day, I announced, "You know, I just can't be an atheist. I just . . . I can say it, but it's just words. I have had too many stories up in the trees, had too many mystical experiences. I certainly understand why you have come to the conclusion to be an athiest, but it isn't my conclusion. I'm not a Christian or an atheist; maybe I'm somewhere in between those, if that space exists."

It had to be the shortest journey of atheism of all time. I didn't even want to tell any atheists for fear of being ridiculed. And I didn't want to tell any Christians for fear of the same. I felt like I had no tribe whatsoever. I had no idea where I belonged in the ever expanding world of belief.

Silence

**I have spoken long enough
I have spoken well enough
Now let me be silent
And see how Silence speaks**

—"Your Silence," Aparna Chatterjee

The voice on the news said twenty children and six adults had been shot. The gunman shot his mother before going to Sandy Hook Elementary School, and in the end he turned the gun on himself. The world ached, like so many times before. Amelie was three years old, and I just couldn't imagine a grief like that. I leaned against her crib that night holding her tight, weeping for all the mothers and fathers who wouldn't get to hold the child they lost that day.

How is it possible to feel it so much when it didn't even happen to me? It happened to them, not me, so why do I feel like I cannot breathe? I watched a documentary about Hiroshima once. I had to turn it off. The narrative told by a mother was too much to hear. It felt like I was in the mother's body, experiencing her grief while hearing her daughter scream as the fire covered her little body up.

"I don't know how to deal with a grief like that."

I told this all to a woman named Ruth while on a silent retreat in Sacramento, desperate to know how to live in a world that holds both beauty and pain. I had never been silent for a single day, let alone five. Never meditated for a half hour, let alone two hours. They used words I wasn't used to, had music playing that definitely didn't belong in the tribe I had come from. My dot had warned me about this music before. We said prayers while moving our bodies in sync with each other, and at the end we would open our arms and say, "I am thankful for everything and everyone." It felt a little reminiscent of my holy-roller wild church, but with different language and Buddha statues.

The only talking that happened was greeting each other in the mornings, and one or two meetings with the hosts. So this is how I came to talk with Ruth. Ruth was an older woman who looked like she'd sprung right out of the forest ground, draped in embroidered dresses and white hair, soft and long. We sat on a cushion, and she asked if there was something I wanted to talk about. "Yes, there is," I said, trying to seem centered and calm like I had been practicing mindfulness for twenty years. I began calmly, "Well, I always felt there was this presence with me, but as I have gotten older, experienced the world, belief has been changing." And then I heard my voice shaking, pleading, "How can you say you are thankful for everything and everyone? I believed so thoroughly before, and now it just feels like my faith is split in two. I tried to be an atheist, but I can't, but it's also incredibly hard to believe in a good God or to understand just what exactly God's role is in all of this. Because I've seen the world. I know what it's really like now! We have the Twin Towers falling, genocide in Rwanda, Isis, priests hurting children, three hundred girls missing, earthquakes in Haiti and beyond, devastation and starvation and loss everywhere every single day. I used to believe there was a God saving all of this, putting it all to right. I believed, I truly believed, and now . . . now I don't know what is going on here. A man just murdered children at Sandy Hook Elementary. Children. So no, I am not thankful. And I really don't think we should be saying we are."

I sat looking at her with tears running down my face, hoping she had a grand truth to reveal.

Her eyes were blue, calm yet tinged a bit red, with tears brimming. But she didn't furrow her brow, didn't flinch. She looked at me the way someone looks at a newborn baby with a slight conehead screaming its way into the world—with love and compassion. Then she looked at me like she was looking into a deep lake of water, not the pleading, angry girl in front of her.

She nodded.

"Yes, I understand." Her eyes glistened. "And therein lies the meditation."

And that was it. Her lips turned up on the corners so slightly. We sat there for a few minutes longer. I blinked. She hugged me and I walked away a little bewildered.

Oh, Ruth, you and your hippy beads, calm demeanor, and beautiful flowing hair, what do you know about suffering?

It turned out she knew a lot. It turned out a calm soul isn't something that just happens. Suffering teaches us. And we learn either to calm or to drown.

We did more prayer movements, more meditation, more listening. Day three was a hard wrestle emotionally, and also because I was eating only raw veggies and my body just didn't like that much health. By day four, I found my body wasn't resisting the movements, only slightly resisting the raw diet. My mind centered during the meditations. I found the knots of frustration began to untie.

On the last day, I was up before dawn. I sat on top of a hill that overlooked vineyards, farms, rolling hills. It was misty and dark. Light slowly rose from behind the hills, glowing deep orange and yellow. Light began to spill over the hills, outlining shapes as it crept. There were fat cows freckling the green, pausing to eat or poop and chat or whatever it is that cows do. Roosters began their daily chant; lights turned on in houses.

I realized that the line I had been running on through early marriage, Michigan, and Denver was shaking. But it wasn't a violent shaking. It was more like how a mother bird nudges her babies out of the nest because she knows what they are meant to do. But I was hesitant. What was I holding on to? What was I attached to? Why did I keep looking back to the dot I came from as my true north?

If Love or God or whatever I wanted to call it was good, wouldn't it hold me if I let go?

I thought about that time with Michael when we opened up our hands to the dream of children, the time I declared atheism. I was creating suffering because I was clenching my fists. I wanted what was in front of me to be different than it was, so I wasn't able to receive the gift of what was.

It seemed like I was holding on to something that I shouldn't have been—my expectation for the world to be free of pain. My expectation for the guy in the sky to swoop in and change things. My attachment to how I believed things should be—what a strong attachment. I looked at my hands, opened them up, finally let go.

I think it was then that I had the first glimpse—how pain and beauty are all part of life. The cows, the rooster, the rolling hills, the people—all of it was just in this process of living. Everything had a place and was part of this thing happening. I felt this comfort, almost like feminine arms holding me, helping me understand Ruth's words about gratitude. My mother always helped me relax as a child, when I was scared and pulled the covers up over my head at night. In this moment, the earth felt like that—a Divine Mother pulling the covers off of my head, encouraging me not to be afraid of the pain of this world and not be afraid of letting go of what used to be my true north. I knew I had been cautious with this retreat because it wasn't centered on my given traditions, but the music, the language, the move-ment—I realized, really, I had been learning this my whole life, how to let go and open my heart. The music made my heart open, just like music had done all along. The words were different; the meaning was the same—open your heart, follow Love. We all come from different parts of the earth. The word for watermelon isn't the same everywhere. Neither is the word for peace or for spirit or for anything else. How did I ever expect it to be? It's all this practice that we do to open our hearts, recognize the divine. I thought this practice belonged to one specific group. My entire life I thought my line was the one true line holding all of the truth. But now I found myself with people of all religions, doing things I never thought I would, like crazy synchronized body movements and two-hour meditations—something the people on my dot would say is "opening your mind to Satan himself." But instead of finding Satan waltzing in and taking over my limbic system, I found love, calming my frantic mind, centering my heart.

I felt it was okay for Michael and me to be on different pages. Life wasn't about struggling to be on the same page but was about seeing the person. It was about seeing what was right in front of me in all of the cow poop and glorious light.

My body unfolded and unfurled as a bright tangerine glow made its way to my feet. And I know I was prepared for something that day—a fall, and a flip of the world that begins to turn everything right side up.

Mother

Our plans never turn out as tasty as reality.

—RAM DASS

We are having another baby!"

I screamed, ran to the sofa with pregnancy stick in hand, and jumped on Michael. I put my face right on his, our foreheads touching and eye to eye. "Are you excited? Scared?!" He stared openmouthed. "Oh my gosh!" he said, putting his hands on his head and laughing, looking quite terrified.

We were leaving on a tour in two days. Not only did we have a three-year-old in tow, but now Michael also would have a sleepy, hungry, sick, hormonal, pregnant person—bonus.

So we did it all again. I called my mother. Again she cheered and cried. We called friends and family, laughing and jumping with excitement. Then we hit the road, and I did all the pregnant-on-tour stuff again—barfing, tossing in the hard bunk, playing shows, crying in the bathroom because I wasn't sure how in the world people had two kids, traveled, and kept their sanity.

My silent retreat in Sacramento sent me on a journey, a practice to see the world with new eyes. Yes, there was work to be done in the world, but there was so much magic I just wasn't seeing—soil, skin, winged creatures in the sky, a sun that keeps us alive, a little girl I made from my body who was growing and seeing wonder in everything. I also found myself discovering the feminine side of God. After all those years of saying God is neither male nor female yet calling him Father anyway, I realized I never actually reflected it in my everyday language. And so my language shifted: "God" became "Divine Mother." I found new language and practices that helped me live from my heart again.

My mantra every day was "Divine Mother, give me eyes to see." I said it in the morning as I meditated, as I changed a diaper, and as I worked. I sat at the piano and wrote a song called "God Our Mother," and Amelie sat beside me as I played. "You know, sweet girl, God isn't a man. He also isn't a woman, but these are just words we use to help us connect," I said to her.

"But . . . I thought God had a penis," she said.

"Nope!" I said.

"So he has a vagina?"

"Nope, no vagina either."

"So what does he have?"

"God isn't 'he,' honey."

"Oh yeah, so what does she have? I mean . . . this is weird."

I wondered why it took me so long to see just how deep ran the patriarchy of our Western society, and in most of the churches. It's in the boardroom and schoolhouse; it's battled in the home and praised in the pulpit. It's in the woman who must learn to "fight like a man" to be successful and the boy who has to toughen up and "don't cry like a girl." The wounds are in everyone, not just the women. I saw it everywhere but always felt it was just the way of the world. I bought into it. I didn't know you could live outside of such a structure—or at least attempt to.

"Mother" feels like a side of God that hasn't only been ignored but purposefully rejected. Maybe it made God feel weak, or too emotional or too caring. There was an uproar years ago about a book portraying God as a black woman. I remember reading that book and crying my eyes out. That side of God was the one I knew as a child, the one I had known all along, but the image got crowded out by paintings of white Jesus and white God holding white lambs. I think I had always felt the masculine and feminine energy of God when I was young, but somewhere along the way, the feminine got oppressed, starved, and she eventually died.

So I woke up every day and prayed, "Divine Mother, give me eyes to see."

We did more shows. I walked up and down hotel stairs to stay in shape and whispered to Divine Mother. We traveled until I was seven months pregnant, then I called it. It was time to sleep in my own bed and puke in my own toilet.

That's when our doctor began to worry. Our girl wasn't growing like she should. Something was up. I wracked my brain for answers, then beat myself up for not knowing.

I saw a specialist for the next two months, biweekly, then weekly.

"Do you see any issues?" I asked.

"Nope, your girl is just fine. She is just small, nothing to worry about," said the doctor.

"Okay, good, um . . . but . . . are you sure?"

"She is just fine. Her heart looks great."

Then came the next doctor's visit. She wasn't getting enough oxygen to her brain. We raced to the delivery room. And then came all the rest—holding her and crying happy tears, her turning blue and their taking her. Then came the nurse with nervous eyes and hands. She tucked a strand of hair behind her ear and began to tell us their concerns about our girl. "She has signs consistent with Down syndrome . . . she is blue . . . something is wrong." Time slowed.

The world flips. I asked for sight, not for pain.

And like a baby being born into the world, I cry because the light is too bright, things are too real. It's like I've found a warm place to land, and then I'm thrown into something that's upside down. I cry because I don't want this pain and I don't know why I'm being prodded, poked, looked at by eyes outside my own body.

I've felt shame here and there—my lack of sports ability in a family of champions, my chubby belly as a kid and flat chest as a teenager, my ignorance and my shortcomings. But even in all of that, I felt at the center of myself that I was good. Even if I don't measure up, I retreat into myself and know that the heart of me is good, and that in itself is a comfort. Sure, I have been ashamed here and there, but I have never felt anything like this.

This is a mother's shame.

My girl isn't what I expected, and this crushes me so hard. I am afraid I'm failing her, have already failed her—my body couldn't give her what she needs. And will I continue to fail her in the future? We are not the couple who can handle surgeries, let alone the therapies she will need. Quite honestly, we are pretty selfish with our time. We travel a ton, stay up way too late, love to sleep in, and are pretty forgetful—two creative types, not the best combination for a structured household.

I'm supposed to be the one to welcome her fully into the world, not catch my breath when I hear a diagnosis. How in the world can I be so blind to my bias?

I retreat into myself and hate the monster I see in my heart. For the first time I see my own heart as a bad thing, a traitor to myself and to her.

I am ripped apart and wounded. And this is not a sublime turn in the story that comes in one single day, no. This is where I am buried, face the demons I never knew. But I know I have been led here because this is where the light comes in.

PART 3

CIRCLE

Then the line shakes. You command your line to be still. But it becomes a wobbly thing, just like your dot did. It seems to be breaking apart, disappearing beneath your feet. You are terrified. You slip. And you fall.

You fall right into something. It's dark and unknown. And so you suspend inside of who knows what because it is darkness. There are muffled voices, but it's like a different language you have never heard, so you grow fearful.

You sit there terrified to move, afraid you will never see your dot or line ever again because they both have been swallowed up by the darkness.

But then something happens. The darkness speaks.

It names all of the things you have been afraid of, and you beg it to stop. It wraps you up like a blanket as big as the night.

It lets you scream and cry, lets you spill all of your anger out. You curse the dot; it didn't do what it said it would do. You curse the line; it fell apart and let you fall.

The darkness just listens. It puts its hand to your cheek when you make your demands. And soon, after you've spilled out all your anger and questions and hurt, you quiet. You look around. It's a struggle at first, blinking and squinting in the dark, tense hands stretched out in front of you to feel your way along. The darkness begins to teach you how to trust your heart when your eyes can't see, and how to let go of the illusion that you ever saw reality in the first place.

So you embrace the darkness, and it is like your body's sight comes to life. You see you are in a circle, and you walk in the darkness, unafraid.

You slowly see the circle light up, with deep tones here, lighter ones there.

There are countless people who welcome you; you had no idea they had been here all along. They had watched you on your dot and cheered you on. They watched as you fell from your line; they were the voices praying for you, but you couldn't understand the prayer.

Until now. Now you can see that your little dot was the tip of a line which is really a circle you have always been within. The dot shook because it wasn't a dot. It was just how you saw it. The line broke because it was never a solid line. The dot and line were just your perspective. The circle was always the reality underneath and around the reality you could see.

Where the Light Comes In (Part 3)

I can still see Rachael's face. I looked back at her on my right. She smiled with tears in her eyes, a knowing smile. I had no idea how I got lucky enough to have her by my side; she gave me an anchor in the spinning room because she understood without a single word. Her brother, Ben, has Down syndrome and autism. She knew the questions my heart was diving into: Will she connect with me? Will she speak? Will her heart be okay? Will she live? Will this life be hard on her?

I saw my mother. She came into the hospital room with a wide smile and water for me. "I just left the room for a minute. She is here already?" She beamed and laughed, then saw my tears, asked what was wrong. I told her the news, and she smiled with a mixture of joy and pain. She hugged me, and I felt like a child again.

My in-laws came in. Momma G hugged me and looked right into my eyes, told me how much our girl was loved. Pappa G took my face in his hands and leaned in so close. "We love this little girl so much," he said. "And she was born into the perfect family."

I remembered meeting them the night Michael taught me how to swing dance in the driveway. I had no idea the kind of people I was meeting that night and how they would help my very body in the future. *Oh, this is what family is about*—support when you crumble, breath when your lungs fail, believing in you when you don't believe in yourself, seeing you at your worst and not only remaining in the room but leaning in. It's scary to let someone in that close.

Bre and Jamie came in and sat by the foot of the bed. My sister stood by me on one side. My doctor and pediatrician came along the other; she'd delivered my first and was with me through my whole second pregnancy and delivery. She leaned in and hugged me so long and fully, I was grateful to have such a kind woman help me guide our girl into the world.

Then Michael came over. He asked everyone to leave, saying he needed a minute with me. He had just spoken with his sister, and he needed to tell me something she had said to him.

He put his hand on me, and it felt so strange because I knew what it meant. He was going to pray, but after the long absence of it, I wasn't sure what to do—join in? Close my eyes? Laugh in shock? I also wasn't sure whether he knew just who he was touching. Did he see the monster rising in me? Was he ashamed with me? Ashamed I had failed our girl?

He laid his hand on my stomach and in tears said, "For you created her inmost being; you knit her together in her mother's womb."

I grasped his hand, and we just sobbed.

"She is fearfully and wonderfully made."

I have a hard time putting words to this moment. It was a great summit in my life. It's like something broke and another reality opened up. I had never seen Michael as I did right then. It was like pain had stripped us down to the bare bones, and we saw a different side of each other, a different reality. It was like waking up during surgery and feeling your guts being ripped out of your body, but afterward feeling more alive, more awake— something that wouldn't have made sense to me before.

The spinning slowed as we held each other on the hospital bed. We were silent for a while. "Where's our girl?" I asked. I just had to hold my girl, that was all I wanted and needed. She was away for tests; thankfully, they let us in to see her. I scooped her out of her bed and put her tiny body on mine. Peace pulsed through my veins. She opened her eyes and all of the spinning stopped. I saw not medical conditions or uncertainty. I was struck with the wonder of this tiny human.

She looked right up at me. I stared and it was like a wide deep pool of something I didn't really have a word for. Mystery? Love? Light? Wonder? If there were a word that encompassed all of that, then that would be it.

I felt my phone vibrate. It was my father. I knew he'd heard the news. I knew he was worried sick. I answered while I held Lucie in my arms.

"Hi, Dad," was all I could get out.

"Hi, honey," I heard him say through tears. "I just want you to know . . . You need to know how much I love this little girl. I love this little girl, I love her . . . She was born into the perfect family. You can do this," and we both just sobbed into our cell phones like we were right there with each other. And I never would have imagined this moment happening between us. In all the times I just wasn't sure whether we would ever understand each other, if we would ever get over all that had happened or just be okay with who the other was, I never imagined we would ever share this sort of connection. Sharing in suffering—it does something to a soul. It's like a beautiful sad piece of music undoing things so our souls are more alive.

Amelie and I sat in the hospital room. She was holding Lucie, and I was watching them intently. The moment Michael and I had alone felt like the first tear in an age-old lens I had bought into about quality of life, about able bodies, about expectations and limitations I never knew I had. I found myself going back and forth, tossed between sight and fear. I looked at Amelie. She was lost in thought, tracing her sister's face with her finger, touching her chest, her nose.

I sat on the hospital bed, worried. *Does she know? Does she know what is happening, and is she sad that her relationship with her will be different than with others? I had "really good" plans, ones involving dance parties and school plays and sisters doing everything together. Oh, Amelie, what do you think of all of this? Are you sad? We planned so much. You kissed my belly goodnight every night. You sang to her and said you would teach her all the things you know. I don't know if she will even make it home with us, and if she does, what will it be like for you and her at school, with friends? Will there be college? Will there be babies? Will Lucie feel so different from you and be disappointed in herself? Will you be disappointed? And if she doesn't make it home, just how do I tell you that?*

My mind ran with worry and fear, and there was a catch in my throat.

"Hey, baby girl, what are you thinking about?" I asked.

She was silent, not yet done looking. She ran her finger over her sister's cheek, over the cannula and wires keeping a constant check for heartbeat and temperature. Then she softly said, "Oh, I was just thinking she is exactly like I thought she would be."

Sight often comes to us in what we don't understand or expect. We suffer, and it unlatches a different perspective.

A collapse of beliefs leads us to the opening of something true. A collapse of social structure leads us to see human essence. A different side of life was being lit up; I was just learning how to see it, struggling with my adult brain filled with definitions and expectations. Amelie saw it already. She wasn't swayed by the chaos because she didn't have a box for it. She saw only what was true.

Names hold so much. They are called out to us every single day, naming our essence. This little life was already a light to two people stumbling, giving us eyes to see what we couldn't before, illuminating the places we were too scared to look. That's how we found her name. Lucie—it means light.

Paper Hearts and Ballerinas

Michael and I sat on an uncomfortable foldout sofa while his parents stood in the corner in the recovery room. Lucie was gone again—more tests. A cardiologist we will soon see on a regular basis walked into the room and explained her echocardiogram. There were two issues with her heart.

Two. The first rare and not related to her having Down syndrome. "It must have come from one of her parents, the gene passed through her family. The surgery is risky," said the doctor.

Oh, God, I gave her a rare heart defect?

Second, somewhat common for Lucie's diagnosis, her heart didn't really have chambers, so all of the blood was mixing improperly, causing low oxygen, causing her to be blue. The first surgery would be in two days, or possibly tomorrow, and the second when she is around six months old.

No, no, no, this is all wrong. This isn't how this day was supposed to go. Next couple of days? Can I just leave with our baby and go home like all of the other people? I'm supposed to hold her and nurse her, not give her over for tests. I'm supposed to put her in her crib with the frayed yellow picture frames above it, not stay here in the cold hospital. We are supposed to go home with our girl. And what are her chances of survival? I need to know her chances.

I didn't say any of this out loud. I just nodded and tried to look strong while holding back more tears.

I already felt weak from just giving birth, my insides wrought and emotions wrung out. With each set of news the doctors brought, it felt like another wave, knocking the breath out of me, stinging my eyes. It felt too harsh. Two heart surgeries? I wanted to argue with him, to tell him to check again. I wished he had it all wrong.

Day two came and Lucie was pricked, wiped down, prepped for surgery. I couldn't let her eat, which felt like I was telling her she couldn't trust me to give her what she needed. She was five pounds at birth, now just above four, her heart no more than two inches thick, valves paper thin. What exactly do you use to repair tissue paper?

Two nurses came to take her. They smiled at me and worked so swiftly I realized how often they do this sort of thing.

Handing her over to a stranger to cut her open was hell. I gave up all control and was left only to wait. How would I wait? How would I stand here and open my hands in this way? I followed as they walked down the hall, then the nurses went through the double doors. The doors closed too fast and hard, and I just stood there looking at my blurry reflection in the stainless steel.

I couldn't believe that reflection was me. I couldn't believe I was here and my girl would be opened up on a hospital bed without me by her side for comfort or to hold her if she had her last moments in this world. Strangers weren't supposed to be there if that happened. It was supposed to be me holding her, letting her know she was loved. I felt helpless.

The waiting room was filled with family—aunts, uncles, grandparents, cousins, all talking and making the time go by. I sat with my heart in knots, imagining a nurse handing over the scalpel, the doctor hovering over Lucie, his hands cutting the tissue-thin aorta, placing a band in her heart, then stitching her back up, and everyone applauding. She was fine.

Then my mind played out all of the other possibilities a mother's brain is capable of imagining—a simple slip of the hand, a mistake. It was exhausting. I had to stop imagining all the worst outcomes. I joined my niece on the floor to play with a puzzle, listened to stories trailing on from family and friends. This family is good, just the people I needed to keep me from crumbling. I needed talking and stories to continue, a piece of normalcy in the chaos.

My mother sat by me, her hand in mine. It struck me that she and I had been here before—waiting in the hospital, hoping for a good outcome. But she was the worried mother when I came two months early. She'd told me the story at least a hundred times—she hemorrhaged; the doctor told my father I would die and she would possibly die, so he should prepare; he might be going home by himself.

She felt life leaving her body, then she remembered someone telling her to call out to God and he would save her. She did, and amazingly, she felt life coming back into her. The doctor made a long cut and took me out of her body; she held my scrawny four-pound frame, held her breath just as I held mine now. This was right where her faith started and solidified—pleading for both of our lives. And somehow, for her, it worked. It set her faith in stone, and there was nothing too big or small, nothing impossible; she just believed. As thoroughly as gravity can be counted on, my mother's faith was steady, certain.

She and I, we had been here before. But after all of the years between then and now, belief looked different. I wasn't certain about what I knew, and she was. I was praying for Lucie's heart to be fixed, but I was wondering whether it was me who was seeing her diagnosis all wrong. Suffering is what happens when we want what is in front of us to be different than it is, and I wondered just how much suffering actually exists versus how much I was creating.

I walked onto a patch of grass outside of the hospital, called a friend, paced in a circle. A row of houses sat across the street from the hospital, but life in the hospital and in those homes seemed worlds apart. On that side of the street, a man cursed at his dog for pooping in the wrong spot; on this side, a father cursed the medicine that just wasn't working on his child. I wanted that side—frustration with dog poop, certain about the trajectory of life. Not this side—surgery and suffering and uncertainty. I walked inside, helped my mother collect her things so she and Amelie could head home for a rest and Amelie's dance recital. I walked the halls. I tried to eat, but it felt ridiculous and selfish to do such a thing while Lucie couldn't. I sat back down in the waiting room chair for someone to give us either the best news or the worst. It was hours later when the doctor walked in. *This is too early*, I thought, trying to read his face. Was he tired? Concerned? Regretful?

"The surgery went well, the best it could," he said, and we all exhaled. "She received a blood transfusion. She is being stitched up now, then we wait for Lucie to wake up."

We cheered. We hugged. I breathed easily for the first time in hours and collapsed in tears of relief. It felt like a cinch had been around my lungs and finally snapped off.

We couldn't go see her just yet. The doctor said they needed to finish the sutures and her anesthesia wouldn't wear off for a few hours. I sank into my chair, relieved, then I remembered something—Amelie had a dance recital in thirty minutes.

I looked at Michael. "Oh, baby, Amelie's recital—this is crazy, but I want to go!" Amelie had been waiting so patiently through so much—even before with appointments and preparing and bed rest. I wanted her to know I saw her. I knew she needed a little cheer in this chaos, and maybe so did all of us. I looked to the doctor. "Oh, everything is fine here. You should go!" he said. "Lucie needs to sleep the rest of the day. She is in good hands."

I thought it would just be us, but all of our family and friends sprinted like a pack of wild animals out of the hospital and piled into cars. I called my mom, and she grabbed Amelie's ballerina outfit, met us outside our house, and we raced to the recital.

We rushed Amelie in, found the teacher, quickly told her the story of why we were late, and she delayed the performance twenty minutes so our family could find parking and seats. Sometimes humanity really comes through.

The other mothers saw me walking with a bit of pain and a much smaller belly as Michael and I made our way to the performance room.

"You aren't pregnant anymore?!" they asked in wide-eyed surprise.

"Oh, yeah, yeah, um . . . It's crazy! I just had her yesterday. She is actually in the hospital right now. She is beautiful! So small, has Down syndrome . . . and . . . had heart surgery. I'm still hurting in my lady parts a lot, you know how it goes . . . But, well, see you in there!"

I realize what a crazed mess I must have looked and sounded. But I didn't care. I just needed this. I needed Amelie to know we saw her. We all found seats, laughed as line of little girls fidgeted and giggled, looking to catch their parents' eyes. Amelie was up, and we applauded the loudest anyone ever has as she skipped, twirled, and sashayed across the wooden floor, glitter trailing from the hem of her tutu.

We tucked Amelie in bed that night and she smiled wide. "Did you see me twirl, Momma?"

"Yes, love, you were amazing!"

"Maybe now that I have a little sister, she will be a ballerina too!"

"Yeah, maybe so." We smiled and I kissed her head. Michael and I made our way back to the hospital, back to wait on Lucie to wake up.

"The next twenty-four hours are crucial," said the doctor. "Her body has been through a lot. This is the time infection can set in, but she is doing good, and we will do our very best."

Wake up, Lucie, just open your eyes once so I can see you are okay.

She looked like a fragile little machine made of metal and skin, something I would see in a movie and say in disbelief, "Oh come on, that looks so fake. Couldn't you make the baby look less pale and less shocking?" She looked like a plastic imposter with tubes and wires covering her little frame like a web. It was difficult to look at her. Seeing the needle in her arm and the tube in her mouth made everything in me hurt. She had bruises here and there, and it all seemed too harsh for anyone two days old. She didn't ask for this, and I wondered whether she was scared of this world already. A machine made her chest rise and fall, breathing for her. Wires went into her abdomen and attached to her heart in case it stopped. "Just in case," the nurse said.

I wondered how many times "just in case" happened.

We waited. We walked to her bed and sang to her, then waited some more.

It felt like it was taking too long; she should be awake by now. I paced the floor, touched her arm. *If you just can't stay in this world, love, if it already hurts too much, I understand, and you can go. But if you can, I would really love for you to wake up.* Her fingers moved. Her mouth tried closing on the tube going down her throat. An eye fluttered. And then they both opened.

What the Night Brings

Listen, are you breathing just a little, and calling it life?

—MARY OLIVER

I heard the beep, steady and staccato. Heard the click and hum of machines monitoring her breathing, the oxygen in her blood, the beating of her heart. Her heartbeat slowed. I stilled my body and listened.

"Come on, little heart, keep going," I whispered. It picked back up.

It was day five. Or was it four? There is no sleeping in a hospital; day and night run into each other. Doctors came in for checkups at all hours of the night. I was blurry eyed, and my mind was swimming when they told me she'd developed a bad infection. They gave her medicine whose name I couldn't pronounce. She had jaundice too, so she lay under a light and wore the tiniest of baby masks to protect her eyes.

I tried not to be upset by this because, come on, she just survived heart surgery at two days old. But recovery was the hard part for her, so I hunkered back down on the bench-bed and covered my head, hiding my tears. A mother in the next room had been here for months. She knew everyone by name. Her daughter was not doing well. She thrashed around and I could hear her cries at night. So I hid because I could not handle the thought of what the other mother was feeling. I could not put myself in the shoes of someone who had held their baby down for tests while she struggled, and I didn't want to be that mother in the future.

I had no answer for why babies get sick. I don't believe we get sick so some guy in the sky can teach us a lesson, but I had always believed we can learn something through it if we keep our hearts open. But in this moment, I didn't want a lesson. I didn't want to keep my heart open or to look for any silver lining, because this was only hard. Reading into it like Lucie was a lesson for *me* felt pretty wrong and selfish. She shouldn't be cut open to teach me something.

There was an entire team of people supporting Lucie. I loved them all. I listened closely for any pause or wavering voice to make sure they were not keeping something from me. *Please, tell me everything. I want to know. I cannot have false hope.* And it felt like I was holding my breath, holding myself together and floating through the halls like a half person.

Rachael brought me coffee, Jodi brought flowers, then Bre and Jamie came in to sit and make us laugh. They held Lucie and ran in the hallway with Amelie, a welcomed reprieve. Amelie and Michael pretended to be doctors with obsessive flatulence, farting over and over again and saying, "Oh! So so sorry, my apologies! So let me take a look at your . . . ohhhh! [more flatulence] Well, how embarrassing! I am quite sorry, it must be the cheese I ate."

Making us all laugh hard. Our days were filled with this, coming in and going out, food, jokes, talking, Amelie bringing life to the gloomy hallways.

But then night came again and I was my worst at night. It was when the monster came back out—fear, uncertainty, the pain. I knew I shouldn't let my mind run wild, but how exactly do you do that when it is your child?

My brain swam with beeps and thoughts of what happened if the beeps stopped.

They were steady. "One, two, three," I counted, and they sped up, then slowed.

Down syndrome—what exactly does that mean? I was given a book and read it cautiously. And here are the conclusions: no one knows what causes it. It begins in the first moments a baby is conceived. Down syndrome, also known as trisomy 21, is caused by the presence of all or part of a third copy of chromosome 21. Chromosomes determine how a person's body is formed and how it functions. The presence of this extra chromosome alters the course of development and creates physical traits such as low muscle tone, almond shaped eyes, a crease across the palm, small body frame. Trisomy 21 carries with it increased health risks and cognitive delays, but the range varies. It is the most common chromosomal condition diagnosed within the United States. *Most common, so why don't I see more people with Down syndrome?* I turned to the next chapter, "Health Risks."

I began reading the long list—heart defects, hearing loss, diabetes, Alzheimers by the age of forty. This made me ache. I read on, stopped at leukemia. *Come on, really?* It all sent me into heavy breathing. *I can't do this, I can't, I can't see my daughter suffer.* Then I looked at my Lucie on the bed. I saw her chest rise and fall in rhythm, those pink lips pursed and moving unconsciously. She was dreaming. I looked at the book again, then to her. Her tiny fingers moved and brushed her face. She lay still and calm. I put the book down.

I know it was meant to prepare me, but the more I read, the more I didn't find Lucie in the pages. It was just information, definitions, facts. I realized our words and definitions do a great job of explaining something complex, but definitions just can't hold the essence of a life. I wondered what it would have been like to give birth to a child with Down syndrome before the syndrome was labeled. Would we be able to see the child instead of the definition? Would I have been so scared? Typical babies don't get a book of lists handed to them on the first day.

"Hey, baby girl, this list? It is not who you are, my love," I said silently, more my soul speaking it to hers. "You are not a list. You are not an outline of concerns or health risks. You are a gift. Perfect. And I know you are going to show us all a thing or two about what it means to live a full life, no matter how many years you get."

I heard the beeps. "One, two, three." I counted them until my head was heavy.

What do I believe?

I believe there is more than what I can see.

I believe Divine Mother is the ocean and I a drop in a wave, so it doesn't really matter if I believe in the ocean. I'm in it and of it. And I believe it's good. I just can't always see it that way.

I believe Lucie's life is a gift. I surely don't want her to suffer, but I don't think having a body with more or less chromosomes grants us suffering or bliss. I have all the typical chromosomes, and I've suffered. I have often felt like a stranger in this world. And what exactly is a good life, anyway? Have I bought into a measurement system that excludes and oppresses? Tells some that their beautiful body is good and others that they are lacking? I hated this thought. I knew I'd bought into it.

I look at Lucie and my idea of a good life is crumbling.

And I'm beginning to see that I am the sick and she the healing.

Measurements

You wake up flawless, post up flawless, flossin' on that flawless.

—Queen B.

Earth can often feel like a stage instead of what she really is—the womb we were born from. It can feel like she turned on us from day one, let all of the people measure us, poke us, test us to see where we fit on the human scale. But I don't think she turned. I think she screamed and yelled to all of us, "Look! Look! Don't you see what I have given you?! If only you could see, maybe you would stop turning your face toward the sky and asking to be blessed! Don't you see that you are? Don't you see that I have?"

I was born two months early and four pounds light, jumped right into the measurements from the word go just like everyone else did. My mother said people would stop her on walks to admire her new little bundle of joy, only to gasp in horror at how gaunt and frail I was after she unveiled my face. My cheeks gained the weight first, and so dawned the nickname "Bug Eyes and Chipmonk Cheeks." My parents did a lot to help me catch up, and I continued having that "catching up" feeling well into high school. I learned quickly there are two kinds of people in the world: winners and losers. I heard sports was supposed to bond people, but I just didn't see that happening, at least not for me. I knew which category I was in, and it wasn't the "winners."

But I found where I belonged in church, not even realizing I was still buying into the winners-and-losers system. It was just the godly version. I got my feeling of belonging from believing I was part of the elite, the ones who had the truth. So everyone else could play sports all they liked; I had the truth of the cosmos in my hands.

There is a chart for almost everyone. Tests for almost everything. So we know exactly where we stand compared with everyone else, so we can know if we are special in this world. Special. How many people have spent their entire lives needing to know they are worth something? Not ever feeling like their lives belong on this life-producing planet.

I have found my own charts. I live with them every single day. So for all of my programmed reasons, I needed to know what to expect, just what the charts were for my Lucie. I sat on the sofa in the hospital and googled "life expectancy for people with Down syndrome."

According to the Global Down Syndrome Foundation, "Today the average lifespan of a person with Down syndrome is approximately sixty years. As recently as 1983, the average lifespan of a person with Down syndrome was twenty-five years. The dramatic increase to sixty years is largely due to the end of the inhumane practice of institutionalizing people with Down syndrome."

I read on about the tests, the lobotomies, the precious lives used for research. I know we are still evolving as humans, but come on, we still eat our own—inhumane practices in the name of progress.

I sat there staring at the hospital wall, wondering what the future would hold for someone like me living in this world of progress. Just how long until my IQ isn't high enough, my body not able enough, my life not producing enough to deem me a valuable human being?

I found myself thinking, *Okay, well, she has this syndrome, but maybe she will be on the high functioning side of it. Oh, God, please, please, please, let her be on the high side!* But the earth spoke back, "Don't you see what she is?" I realized I was buying into the same garbage I was fighting.

I wanted Lucie's life to be valuable. But I have ill-defined what valuable is.

And this idea comes only because I have felt this in myself. We have all felt it: our value lies in our able-ness. It lies in whether we wow someone with our ability or disappoint them with inability. We are the tree ashamed of its branches. We have bought into this idea that our bodies and lives need to measure up to something. But when I look at my girls, I already see it— pure beauty. If you were to hold yourself as a baby in your arms, you surely wouldn't have some of the ideas you now have about yourself. I think you'd see things differently. I'm sure my mother looked at my chubby naked baby body and loved every inch. And now, I can stare at my naked self and see so many flaws, shrink in disappointment at what isn't big enough or small enough or just what wobbles when I don't want it to.

"She is so behind." Or, "She is doing so well!"

According to which measuring stick, exactly? To what we "civilized" humans think thriving is?

Our measuring stick is limited to the able, the sound of mind, and the healthy. And so we have people swarming the measuring stick, wondering whether they stand out, fit, belong at all. The game is played everywhere.

In the future, I will visit schools, looking for a good place for Lucie to thrive. I will leave many of them telling myself to breathe deeply; others I will leave with hot angry tears. I'll text my husband, "Hell hath no fury like a woman scorned." He will laugh and say, "I'd be afraid if I were them."

It will be after the fourth private school and the third public school furrow their brows and say there really isn't a place for Lucie that I will stop and realize something.

The system isn't broken. The system was built this way.

Like when I discovered that my father had had pennies in his pockets, I'll feel tricked by this system. They had been so helpful with my "typical" child, excited when they found out she was so bright and tall and talented. They had a place for this beautiful tree to grow taller, better. I won't be prepared for the pain I'll feel when the head is shaken no at our Lucie. I'll think they must not understand. "No, no, she is an actual child. I see other children running around. Well, she too is an actual child. Look! See?"

And I'll walk away feeling the unfairness of it all. Lucie will be put into a category and not even given a chance, the beautiful tree shoved into the shadows with rationed sunlight and water.

It makes me think about all of the other children who were never given a chance. All of the people with illness or physical difficulty, the mothers and fathers who face racial discrimination, and I'm just now getting a little taste of bias. My anger was then turned toward myself because I never saw it to this degree. I didn't know how hard it still was. I knew the bias was there, but there was a big difference between knowing and experiencing this crushing feeling—a frown directed at my child, disapproval for how she was born. I never fully knew it because my skin is light and my body able. But now that I have something deemed to be different, I see the bias more clearly. I was angry at myself for not seeing this before.

I thought about all of the other families, all of the mothers and fathers who had walked this road before me, way before me, with less finances, less help, less social status, less of everything. They had no one to help them and their child was turned away because our system was built on eugenics.

No, it isn't broken. It was built this way.

We separate ourselves in more ways than one with categories and definitions. Politically, socially, racially, religiously. Disabled, mentally ill, genius, dull. This syndrome and that one. It may help with organizing things, helping us know how to help, but our categories most often blind us. We categorize the smartest so they can get smarter faster. So that the "slow" children do not hold back the "shining stars." We teach our children who is "normal" and who is "different." And this alters the development of their reasoning. We are hurting them in the endeavor to make them better.

We are teaching them that the slower learners or those who learn in a different way don't matter as much, that the fastest, strongest, smartest matter most, and this creates a society built on an erroneous idea of success. It creates a society where people feel valued not because they are human beings but because of how well they measure up and produce.

And so we buy in to the illusion that the human experience is best in able bodies, quick minds. We buy into the illusion that we should dominate, then those who dominate are left empty, wondering if they are worth anything more than their winnings. There is a difference between pursuing your best self and pursuing domination. One enriches everyone; the other oppresses everyone.

Jean Vanier wrote, "A society which discards those who are weak and nonproductive risks exaggerating the development of reason, organization, aggression, and the desire to dominate. It becomes a society without a heart, without kindness—a rational and sad society, lacking celebration, divided within itself and given to competition, rivalry, and, finally, violence."

This is not our apocalyptic future; this is our present. This is not a "what if"; this is reality today.

Approximate abortion rates for babies diagnosed with Down syndrome in utero:

United States: 70 percent
Holland: 74 to 94 percent
Canada: 80 percent
Great Britain: 90 percent
Denmark: 98 percent
Iceland: 100 percent

Herein lies a deep ache—to see my daughter's value denigrated by statistics.

And to me, the worst thing about those numbers is seeing someone react to hearing that some of those children who were aborted did not have Down syndrome. They gasp in horror. "No, no, not a 'normal' child! How tragic!"

Just what have we reduced the human experience to? What about empathy, compassion, love? How do you quantify those qualities? Research shows that when children with a wide range of IQs are together in a classroom, everyone's test scores rise. Living and learning alongside each other enriches all of us.

But our country was built on separation, built on the backs of slaves, violence toward native people, sexism, patriarchy—people oppressing people. Rewarding violence and oppression with more power. Some of us thought the civil rights movement would bring change. Some of us thought *Brown v. Board of Education* would bring change. Some thought having a black president would bring change. I know I did. But the impulse to categorize runs deeper than we knew. Our measurement system is a strong one. And now white supremacists proudly show their faces. Iceland is eradicating children with Down syndrome, eugenics happening right before our eyes.

All under the banner of creating a better world, a place where the elite feel like they belong and thrive with the other elite. We cut pieces of ourselves off hoping to save ourselves, not realizing we are bleeding out.

The Earth spins, sleeps, then wakes again and asks, "Don't you see who you are? Don't you know you are good?"

I'm trying to know it. It's a struggle sitting there in the hospital, looking at the charts, seeing where Lucie is compared with all of the other babies. I believe she is perfect, but years of programing are fighting my heart. The programing says, "You should be scared. Her life will be hard. Do every single thing you can to help her fit in. If you fail, shame, shame, shame."

Just what are we looking at here? Those trees, this grass. I could map the intricate patterns in the bark, trace the rings from the center to its edge and make a chart of it. I could measure them and tell each and every one about my findings so they'd know what I know—just what they are.

The wonder of it isn't enough. We have to write it down and take some measurements.

Maybe if I could catch one of those winged wild blue birds, I could study its feathers and feet. Catch another and compare. Then tell them the differences between each other so they can really know what they are and we can know the difference.

The problem is I don't think they would really care. So first, I'd have to teach them how to care about such a thing.

What is it that taught us? Capitalism? Maybe that would work for them too.

I'm not lobbying to burn all the charts. Some are quite useful. I used one last week to find out whether I need glasses. My friend used one to know how much chemotherapy she needs to survive, and my father used a chart to know whether his heart could last. But the charts that compare us, separate us—those are the killers.

It seems the trees are doing okay without my telling them which is thriving more than the other. I wonder what that knowledge would do. Would it push one to be greener? Stand out? Be taller than the rest so it can be closer to the sun? Would it make the other wilt or stunt its growth because the light is blocked, the soil sucked dry from all of the best roots growing so deeply and wonderfully?

Can a tree feel insignificant? Just where did we learn the measureents, and when did we forget we grew out of the ground just like everything else? Do we feel the connection to all of this? If we did, maybe we wouldn't be combining chemicals that rip it all to shreds or making charts to tell us how we don't belong in the very womb that created us.

Going Home

The "night sea journey" is the journey
into the parts of ourselves that are split
off, disavowed, unknown, cast out,
and exiled to the various subterranean
worlds of consciousness. . . . The goal
of this journey is to reunite us with
ourselves. Such a homecoming can be
surprisingly painful, even brutal. In order
to undertake it, we must first agree to
exile nothing.

—STEPHEN COPE

We packed up everything in our hospital room. Today was the day we got to go home.

I tucked Lucie into a car seat that seemed way too big for her five-pound frame. I'd rather put her in a bubble, and though I was excited to leave the hospital, I was also scared.

"You sure we are okay to take her home? I mean, she just had heart surgery, and her feet are blue."

"Just call us or come right back if her lips or body turn blue. Give her this amount of this medicine, that amount of that one."

"Um, okay. So which shade of blue are we talking? And how am I supposed to sleep at night? Do we take shifts to make sure she doesn't turn the bad shade of blue?" I looked to Michael, and we both looked a little unprepared. We knew CPR, but that's about it in the medical arena. It doesn't seem enough for a baby who was hooked up to a breathing machine two weeks prior.

I think the only thing that stopped me from drinking all the alcohol and taking all the drugs to numb my fear was that I was breastfeeding. Getting your baby drunk or high is kind of a faux pas.

We hugged nurses and doctors. We cried and thanked them profusely. They had saved our girl. And I wasn't quite sure how you thank someone for such a thing. "Thank you" seems too short, too shallow. We waved goodbye to our little room, the hallways, the little bench-bed I'd spent the last two weeks sleeping on. Rachael videoed us as we left for home.

When we got home, we walked inside, dropped our bags, and said, "Look, Lucie girl! This is your home!" We showed her to her room. I showed her the yellow frames above her crib. She was thrilled, of course. She let out a tiny sigh which I took to mean, "Oh, this is the best thing ever! Thank you for your ever-abundant feng shui skills, Momma." I felt like we had way too many things for this tiny baby. We had mounds of toys, a swing that rocked itself, five different kinds of swaddling blankets, a dozen different vitamins, and books and music that were sure to make our baby the smartest ever. But all we really needed was one tiny little spot to lay her down among the three of us.

Michael, Amelie, and I put her on the bed and dove into

baby-talk blabber. Being home felt so sudden, like we were returning to this regular world all too fast. The beeping of the machines was gone. The endless troops of nurses to help—gone. The calm was nice, but then I panicked a little now that it was up to just the two of us.

I checked her feet. Slightly blue. Should I call the doctor? I decided to wait. I promptly called. They told me she was fine.

Evening came and Michael and I tucked the girls into bed— Amelie on the left side of the room, Lucie on the right.

I kept checking on them to make sure Amelie didn't scoop her sister out of the crib for a midnight doll party, and to make sure Lucie was actually breathing. "We have two kids. I can't believe we have two," I said while curling up close to Michael on the sofa.

It felt like our hospital stay had gone by so slowly, and now that we were home, it felt like we had just left for the delivery room. We watched the video we took on our phone as we left for the hospital. We were smiling, packing things up and waving to my mother, certain of our plans. It was like watching different people. We were so oblivious then, so certain we would be coming home without medicine or heart surgery or major change.

We came home as different people. It was like I was in the home of a family we used to be, an idea we used to have. Everything looked familiar, but it all belonged to other people, different parents than the ones sitting here on the sofa.

"I can't believe this has happened."

"I know," Michael said, half asleep. "But you know, I just . . . I feel like we got lucky," I said. "I'm seeing this other side of life I didn't know before."

"Yeah, I feel the same," Michael said.

Michael and I were in a full body hug on the sofa. We nodded off.

But each day was very much "three steps forward, two steps back." I would feel myself breaking into this whole new view, then fear would claw its way back in and reposture my body to be afraid of health issues with Lucie. A few days after we came home, I was sitting on our bed doing laundry while Lucie made tiny sounds and Amelie played. Michael's phone rang, and after a while he hung up, looking weak. The friend we brought on to pastor the church in Denver didn't want us there anymore. And I regressed. I did not feel lucky.

As the friend's reasons unfolded, I became angry, hurt. This was the place our family needed most right now, the place I needed most. The timing was like a bad joke.

We tried to find common ground with the friend who wanted us out, wondered where it had all gone wrong, were determined to work it out. Then I opened bills and my lungs constricted even more. We took a walk with our friends, Bre and Jamie; yes, fresh air could help take our minds off of the bills and drama. We ended up running into two parents. I noticed the man staring at Lucie like he saw a ghost. Bre tried to coax him out of his stupor, but like a tranced thing, he told us he had a daughter with Down syndrome. She had leukemia, was better now, but it was so difficult. He just kept saying, "It was so hard," staring wide eyed at Lucie. I silently crumbled. Bre instantly jumped in with "Oh, we are so sorry. Glad she is better. See ya later." And she ushered me out of the room into the hallway, where I broke down in sobs. "I can't do cancer with a child. I'm not strong enough for that . . . Did you see his face?"

It was like a valve I'd closed off with positivity and sight opened again and out gushed fear about Lucie's future—how long she would live, what sicknesses she could get, question after question unearthed. And there was fear about us—were we actually terrible people? What about inclusivity? What about love in the toughest times? Why did our friend want us out?

Over the next few days I stopped changing clothes. I slept in whatever I had on and wore it the next day, then the next. All of the wonderful profound enlightenment I experienced dimmed in the wake of no sleep because of keeping a tiny human alive, clean, fed, not blue, leukemia-free. The light faded in facing the fact that no amount of preparation or vitamins or positive thoughts would save Lucie's life or save us. Control was an illusion.

In passing I noticed my reflection in a mirror and I stopped. "This is me, this is . . . me, real life," I told my reflection.

I didn't know who this girl was. She was unkempt and crazy eyed. I didn't like her very much. I saw someone who was failing, someone who couldn't hold herself together, change clothes, or even keep her hair combed. Where had all of my positivity gone? The feeling of being lucky? The sight?

That next morning I found myself unable to get up, and the next morning after that. I nursed Lucie and cried, pretended to smile when Amelie came into the room, then cried. I got the news that a friend had delivered a healthy baby girl. I knew she didn't even want her, and it made me so angry I didn't know what to do with myself. I had never experienced this sort of sadness, the kind where your mind and body feel like they have given up.

You can promise them all the things in the world if they just get up, but they have lost their desire for anything, so promises are futile. You can tell it all the good things that are happening and just what you should be grateful for, but it doesn't work. I felt I was failing as a mother. I couldn't keep myself together. How would I give anything good to my two girls, and just how could I give a thing to my husband? I wondered if he'd find a better girl, one who combs her hair and doesn't smell bad. Maybe this new girl could clean my house and feed my family. That would be nice.

One morning I heard music coming from the other room. I could see Michael through the doorway. He was singing and playing the piano. Tears were on Michael's face, his posture the way posture is when you are worn out all the way through. It felt good to hear him sing, to feel the music wrapping us up. I dragged myself to the sofa while holding Lucie. We let the sound of the piano warm us. We let our sadness spill out.

On the two opposite sides of health, nothing means anything. On the worst side, it means nothing because you are attached to how you think things should be and so you suffer. On the good side, it means nothing because you have realized your reality is false, your attachments are gone, and you are free. I was very much attached, very much enraged with the world and who I was. It was paralyzing.

This was where I found myself in the chase, driving fast to get away from the invisible monster. This was where I was screaming like a crazed wild thing while the person in the car next to me stared terrified at the phycho woman on Interstate 25.

Ten minutes previously, Michael had suggested we both take a breath. We'd switch off, each taking a day in the mountains. He said he thought I should go first, and I didn't even politely reply with "oh, no, honey, you go first." I was out the door in minutes, a change of clothes and a breast pump in hand.

I drove white knuckled and heavy footed, our black Jeep's engine roaring as I sped up and passed two cars I was mad at for driving so slowly. I turned on the song "Land of the Living," which played when Lucie was born, and recalled each moment of her birth. I was angry that children have to have surgery, angry that the world is this way, angry that I was a wimp for my older daughter instead of strong like all of the other she-warrior women I saw on social media. I knew life isn't fair and I knew it would be hard, but never this hard. And I was mad that this is the hard part for me.

The surgery worked. I should be relieved. The bills mean there is hope, that there are surgeons who have the skills to do this work. But I had come unglued somehow, and my lack of strength made me angry with myself. Somehow all of this unlatched a beauty that I had never seen before, but also a monster I hadn't known existed.

Maybe I'm trying to make meaning where there is none. Maybe it's just hard and there is nothing to learn.

Maybe we should run to the mountains and live wild and naked, free from bills, etiquette, racism, sexism, ableism, walls of houses, and wifi. The trees don't live that way, so maybe we should live with them.

Maybe I'm just really a terrible person and mother and will never get it right. Maybe the world will never get it right either. Just who will break Lucie's heart and who will really see her?

And who will really love me if they know all of my secret thoughts? I know what rejection feels like. I know what it's like to live in a world where you have to measure up, man up. I don't want her to feel this, so let's run.

I passed cars. The same song had played three times. I played it again, and the voice rang out, "Lay your soul on the threshing floor."

I didn't want the damned threshing floor. I wanted something else. Anything else, really.

I didn't want to leave Colorado. We'd put blood, sweat, and tears into this dirt, worked tirelessly to build something we'd hoped was good. Our community and weekly practice fueled my life in a way that nothing else did. This was it for me, Coloradans for life.

But here was a curve in the road, and I just wanted to keep going straight ahead. No detours, please, and no more hard lessons. I wanted to feel comfort, the warmth of years of walking through the same front door, having the same friends, going to the same annual parties. I wanted familiarity and plenty of money and happiness, and I wanted my kids to be safe and healthy and have bodies that helped them succeed in this world. But what is success? Isn't it to be present and grateful for each moment? I thought about Ruth, about moving our bodies in tandem while giving thanks for everything and everyone. I wasn't thankful for this.

I drove until the grass got tall and I saw a lake. I pulled over and walked to the edge, sank into the grass, looked down deep under the surface.

Why did I feel so scared?

I'd felt so much love in the hospital when Michael prayed, it was like I had peered beneath the floorboards of it all—doubt, faith, reality. What about all of that? Why was it still difficult? I'd seen the truth. Why couldn't I see it now?

I looked into the silvery water, my reflection muddled. Then I looked to the calm beneath. Maybe I was living on the surface, feeling each wave fully because I lived in circumstance instead of something deeper, wiser. I sat there and let time pass, stared at myself like an enemy, grew indifferent, then got up and continued toward Grand Lake.

I rented a canoe at a shabby dock off a dirt road, slid out onto the water, and lay flat on my back in the bottom of the canoe, looking up at the blue sky. It made me remember when I was a kid lying flat-backed on the trampoline, gazing up at the dog, a dragon, or an elephant cloud in the sky, wondering what was beyond my little dot on the map. Ripples rocked me to sleep. I woke later to the crack of fireworks.

I had forgotten it was the fourth of July. It made me think about my mother because it's her favorite holiday. She loves our country and goes all out on red, white, and blue decorations to celebrate. As a child, she celebrated every holiday with gusto— except for Halloween, because it belongs to Satan. She believes our country was built on truth and God. I used to see it that way but now think differently. We've fought about it until we were blue in the face, and I suddenly felt like all of those fights were a bit of a waste. I missed her. I wondered if we would ever see eye to eye on politics and religion and just what God should change in this world. I climbed out of the canoe and sat atop a rock while fireworks burst overhead, reflecting in lakewater as black as ink spilled out wide. They were so bright and loud, they shook my whole body. Stunning how such beautiful bright light could make such a sound, how it could dazzle and also shake me.

Singing in the Dark

**So the darkness shall be the light and the
stillness the dancing.**

—T. S. ELIOT

Have you seen this?" my brother texted.

The picture was of Michael and me. The headline read,
"You Won't Believe Who Doesn't Believe the Bible Anymore."

I laughed and texted back something like, "Oh, wow, where
did you dig that up?" I thought one of our bandmates had
mocked it up as a joke.

But messages and calls started coming fast. One headline
turned into more, and we quickly realized we were in for it.

The first time we came to this lake, we were both eighteen.
It was his first time inviting a girl, and I was anxious that my
two-piece looked too much on the sexy side instead of the pure
side I was trying to stay on.

While I was excited, I was a little bit nervous to be on his

159

family vacation. I hoped they would still like me after I cut their son off on the go-cart ride, and I hoped I would still like them after being in close living quarters for a week.

Mornings quieted the water. Fog hovered out easy on its surface. Evenings brought music and swimming in the cove. Michael and I jumped on the paddleboat and made our way around a bend where no one could see us kiss and talk. More kissing, less talking. The summer air was warm and the insects loud. We were two college kids on summer break, no cares in the world, wildly in love.

So now, it was surreal looking out on the water again— sixteen years of life spread out from moment to month to years with weddings, graduations, new homes, new babies. The kids who once ran across the deck now had kids doing the same. That suddenly felt so strange.

What a thing it is to realize you are the grown-up. You are the adult lugging around kids on an inner tube, the rule setter or rule breaker, the hand that molds summer adventures. You hold the keys to the stories they will tell their friends, significant others, or kids of their own in years to come. I looked out at the water. It all seemed to go so fast.

Were we doing a good job or screwing the whole thing up? I thought I'd have a better handle on life this far in.

The issue with our friend at church hadn't resolved; he wanted us to leave. We were on different forks of a road that had split when I said we needed a rainbow flag at our church and Michael confessed his unbelief—two big no-nos in Christianity. Though we felt our hearts were open and moving forward, our friend was done with what felt like the crazy town of our lives. We couldn't define what we believed, and that obviously makes things difficult for a pastor. Some people wanted us to go; some wanted us to stay. So in the hope of not dividing the church, hurting more people, or seeing it die completely, we felt we had to give it up and move.

Lucie needed therapy a crazy five times per week, so traveling a lot with our band wasn't an option for us anymore. Without touring, living in a musical city seemed vital, plus Michael wanted to get into more composing and scoring, so we figured we would give LA a good ol' college try.

"Cash buyers!" said our realtor.

They wanted to move in quickly. We packed up the last of the dishes and scribbled "kitchen" on the box with a thick marker. Everything else was in storage, then the day of closing, the phone rang, and I knew when I saw Michael's face that the buyers had backed out.

We lay on our empty bedroom floor staring at a white ceiling, reminding ourselves to breathe. It would cost a lot to move all of our stuff back into this home, then out again once we found new buyers. "It's okay, it's okay, we've been through heart surgery. Don't sweat the small stuff," we said. "Let's make it an adventure."

So we stayed two weeks with friends, then with parents, and then we rushed off to the lake house.

I took a breath. It felt good to have distance from the hospital and the issues in Denver, good to have a place of rest while we waited for our home to sell and for Lucie's next surgery.

We unpacked our bags, and that is when I received the text from my brother.

And comments came rushing in.

"I thought I could trust you!"

"I can't believe you lied to us!"

"Repent!"

"Michael is a twofold son of hell!"

"Gungor eats baby seals!" (I'm thinking this one was a sarcastic retort to all of the drama.)

We had been honest—honest about our questions, honest about the moment on Cherry Street more than a year ago when Michael confessed his disbelief, honest about how some days we believe, then some days find it impossible. We'd spoken about it in interviews, in our songs, with anyone who was interested. But some people didn't know any of that, so they felt lied to and tricked. And we were given labels—liars and filthy sinners leading people straight to the fires of hell. I wanted to say, "Well, first off, I don't believe there is a lake of fire, so maybe the next argument is futile?" The controversy spun out.

While Michael fought for clarity and for our future, I walked out onto the deck wondering what sort of jobs or careers we needed to switch to. It looked like we were going down. It also felt like we deserved it. It is quite a strange feeling to be on the "inside" all of your life, then suddenly to be out. I wanted to say, "Oh, no, no . . . Look! See? I am a real human with a heart too! I'm running toward truth just like you are. Let me tell you about it on Twitter with 140 characters!"

It felt like I was suddenly doing the same thing with myself as I was with Lucie when people did a double take and recognized her syndrome—"No, no, look! See?! She is a real-live magical human too, and so am I!". I wanted to fill them all in on the struggle and countless prayers so they would understand.

I wanted to let them know where I was now, but where I was would probably add fuel to the fire. "You're upset I don't think the world was created in six days? Oh, well, honey, let me tell you what else I believe."

We can't see what we can't see. Sometimes it is because we are trying to scream at each other from different stages of consciousness, like a dot to a line. And sometimes it's because we just aren't close enough to see each other. Maybe we should all lean in.

Mind lost in the future, I stared out at the lake, trying to ignore the beeping of our cell phones. A thought lingered: peace doesn't come from circumstance. It snapped me back to the lake-house deck and the thick Missouri air. I was here at the lake to give attention where attention was needed.

There was something waiting—my girl, Amelie, with her flip flops and big blue eyes like two shiny worlds. She was patiently waiting for me to jump into the water with her. She so often waited patiently for me to get unstuck from the grown-up world. In the hospital, we made games out of paper cups, used milk storage containers for her own little medical-supply bag. She pretended to be the doctor and did her regular checkups on the stuffed animals and guests. But after a while, she was just patiently waiting for life to go back to normal.

It was night. I like the idea of swimming in the dark, but I'm always wondering what I'm swimming right above, what might come up to brush my feet or what swamp monster might take me under. Yes, parts of my brain are still five years old.

I wished someone was over there to reach a hand out of the darkness, to tell me where the corners of the walls were and to find the doorway out. If I knew, maybe the dark wouldn't be so bad. It made me remember a time when I hiked up to an avalanche of rocks above Chitawqua Park. I sat in the treeline looking over Boulder, then heard some girls stop short at the avalanche line. "Oh, we can't cross here. This is the end of the hike," one girl said. They all turned around, disappointed that they couldn't keep hiking up the mountain. I decided to call out from my hidden perch, "Oh, it's safe. You can walk across the boulders. They will hold you. I've done it dozens of times. There are actually people on the other side. Look! See?" I pointed to some hikers above us.

With that assurance, they easily crossed and journeyed onward. All it took was knowing it was okay on the other side. All it took was someone reaching a hand out of the darkness and guiding the way.

I grabbed Amelie, ran down to the dock, and we jumped into the dark water, the deep part. We came up laughing and screaming and clinging to each other. I dove under again, faced the darkness. I let out all of the air in my lungs so that I sank beneath the surface, suspended in the calm. My body relaxed. I came up and broke the surface of the water, looking into the night sky, then out at the expanse of watery blackness with the moon painting the ripples wide and far.

Michael walked down the path with sleeping Lucie and a guitar and sat on the dock. And we sang like we always do when life throws a curveball, when we are happy, or sad, for any reason and no reason.

That night, I sang because my heart needed to feel at home and because I needed to do something physical to protest the rising noise. I decided to sing and splash around instead of doing what my emotions wanted—to throw a fit, then have an eternal nap.

Amelie's wide eyes and child voice were right up close. Our noses touched. Amelie laughed.

"Spin with me, Momma! Spin!" We twirled in the water with our faces looking straight up to the stars.

Raising children can lead you to the tortured state of sleep deprivation and locking yourself in the closet just to relive that long lost memory of personal space. But more so, they pull us to the present.

Amelie did that for me that night in the water. She didn't care at all about tribalism. She was blind to social status because she was spinning and laughing hysterically in the middle of a deep blue wonderland where water and sky were inseparable. She was seeing the present, drinking it in. She made me drink as well. All that surrounded us was suddenly more alive, humming and dancing in a cosmic rhythm.

We twirled and splashed as the guitar lines that eventually became the instrumental section of our song "Light" went on.

We walked back to the house, took off our wet swimsuits, and let our hair drip dry. Mine was still drying on my pillow around midnight when the phone went off. It was our neighbor John. Paul had fallen down the stairs, ruptured his pancreas. He was in the hospital, and they weren't sure whether he would make it. Then a few hours later, Paul was gone. I buried my face in my pillow, lay awake most of the night hating such a painful world that just keeps taking.

Solidarity

We stood around the back yard, lit our candles. It was a circle of flickering light landing on faces and hands and dancing in the corners of our eyes.

Our close friends, Michael's parents, and my mother were there. It was the night before Lucie's second heart surgery. I needed to feel their connection, to say prayers, gather with love for Lucie, and stand in solidarity with all the other children and adults with special needs.

I was grateful to have these friends, this family. Previously we'd hidden out at the lake for two weeks, then headed out on tour for a month. We traveled across the country with two girls in tow, playing shows. I pulled myself together many times over, told myself to be a grown-up. "People start over all the time." I lay awake some nights missing Paul, replaying the day I walked into his kitchen and he kissed Lucie's face, told me she was perfect. I thought about Paul's front porch and what it must be like without him there. But how could this be? I needed him there. I needed to tell him about all of this and my diving into the dark water at the lake. I needed him to be there after tour, to place Lucie's feet on the bike pedals like he did with Amelie. It wouldn't be right without him.

We finished the tour exhausted, headed back to Denver to

our still empty house. We set up an air mattress on the floor, then headed over to our friend's back yard just to be present with each other before Lucie's big day.

Amelie lit the first candle, then others were lit, spread out like fireflies hovering in a wide circle. My mother grabbed my hand and I leaned into her.

I wished Paul could be in this little circle with a candle, help me hand Lucie over, because thinking about her being cut right down the middle of her chest was just too much.

Michael was on the other side of me, and I held his hand tight. The last candle was lit, and we said a prayer for Lucie and all of the other families and people who have walked this road. Then we let silence sit with us for a moment. I thought back on the day we moved to Denver in that blizzard and how I held my hand out the window to feel the snow fall. We never know what is coming down the road for any of us. We never know what saying yes to that thing in our gut will do for ourselves or for people we don't even know. I looked at all of these people who had trickled into that little basement throughout the last eight years, how little decisions from ancestors and strangers led us to make our own little decisions and big changes, and somehow we were all now standing here together holding candles. What a wild thing. And what would each of these people face in the future with their own friends and children? Would we do this once again, only in different states, harder circumstances?

We had asked people via social media to join with us in lighting candles, so some started posting photos of our little circle, tagging them #lucieislight, and soon our circle grew and grew. Emails flooded in from families holding up candles. We read their stories in amazement. People all over the country, even the world, were lighting candles of their own, sharing their stories, joining us in solidarity.

The next morning, Michael held Lucie and walked up and down the hospital corridor, singing and whispering to her. I still don't know all he sang or said. I never wanted to ask. It seemed like it was between a daddy and his girl. I fidgeted with her tiny hospital gown, pulled her socks up. A nurse came in and we handed Lucie over. Again I saw myself reflected in the shiny steel doors like six months before.

Her chest was opened up while we waited and paced. Once again, I thought about the worst. I felt I was letting her down by not being by her side and holding her hand. My girl—did she feel my absence? Was she afraid of this world, wondering where the other part of her had gone?

Hours passed, the surgeon came out, taking his hat off as he walked and looked at the ground. Once again, I strained to read his face, whether it was good words or bad he was coming to deliver. "The surgery went well, as good as it possibly could," he said. We once again cheered and cried. And once again, she woke up, this time with about 60 percent more energy. Her tiny heart had been working so hard, and now it didn't have to because it had actual chambers built in it. She woke up kicking and moving like a child who hadn't just had heart surgery but was ready to run at everything.

Friends welcomed us back into their home so our girl could heal up before we embarked to Los Angeles.

A month later, I do my rounds of goodbyes with everyone we know, but there is one last person I have to say goodbye to.

Paul's funeral was a month ago, so it feels wrong knowing he won't be there to greet us as always. Rachael goes with me, and tears come as we approach our two houses. So many moments suspended between the two like a tether.

Others can drive by and just see structures, just bricks and mortar, crooked steps. But me—I see stories. And I see myself changing in ways I never knew I would.

I see Amelie learning to ride her bike on those cracked sidewalks. I see Michael standing in the doorway as rain pours down in the fall. I see parties and baby showers and nights Michael and I are wrapped up in each other's arms on the sofa. I see our marriage bend in places, strengthen in places, aging as we find out what love really is. I see John and Paul on their porch, welcoming strangers, yelling at the solicitors. I see us celebrating with friends, mourning losses. I see my labels and perspectives on just about everything changing. I don't just see houses. I see all of these moments like ghosts lingering about for nostalgia's sake.

I see us walking up the path of risk, parenthood, success, failure, the path that has led us to the doorstep of a second life. I have changed so much here. And it feels like I am leaving the first part of my life behind, now walking into something I don't know yet.

When we dream about our lives, they are often filled with grand ideals—dreams of changing the world, making our remarkably distinct and ingenious imprint on people, maybe even getting a newspaper mention or a plaque or, better yet, an entire banquet with people applauding our impeccable charity and goodwill to all. I've wanted that. I've wanted everyone to know what a great person I am. What an ego game.

But I've found that my life is built on ordinary days of going in and coming out, waking and sleeping, doing dishes, morning coffee, kids playing, running, and leaves turning from green to golden to brown. This is where I've found the grandness. This is where I've found what I believe about life and where I've found myself applauding others instead. It's in long nights on a good porch, letting the silence sit next to you. It's in the hard things that hit or the people who teach, giving you eyes to see.

Paul taught me how to be a part of the lives playing out right next to mine. He didn't tell me about vulnerability or how to walk through pain; he lived it with me. The people I met in this house and in this city did that too.

Rachael and I ugly cry when we get back into her car. We say "goodbye for now." We pretend we'll be living in the same city within the next six months to make ourselves feel better. We know our paths are going in different directions. She is off to San Francisco and we to Los Angeles. It is the close of so much.

It was in this shabby neighborhood in Denver that my definitions and lines were challenged, then erased. It was where I saw Paul showing me the face of God more than any pious man.

What I would give to sit with him on his porch again, tell him about my day, and hear him curse like a sailor.

If I could, I would say this:

"Today I changed a couple of diapers, played with Amelie and Lucie. You should see them. They're getting so big so fast. Sometimes I cry because I'm so in love with them and my body just doesn't know what to do with so much love but cry. It's a strange thing. Then sometimes I cry because being a mother is the hardest thing I've ever done. Yesterday I locked myself in the bathroom just to be alone, but the little one's tiny fingers shimmied under the door in an effort to reach me. It was like a scary movie, but the monster has a really cute face. Life has changed so much. You'd be proud.

"I'm telling people the tiniest piece of your story in a book I'm writing. Imagine that.

"I miss you.

"I love you.

"I'm sorry about the tools I lost.

"And thanks for the whiskey."

Weakness

**We don't know what to do with our
own weakness but pretend it doesn't
exist . . . How can we welcome fully
the weakness of another if we haven't
welcomed our own weakness?**

—Jean Vanier

It was winter when we rolled up to our rental home in Lala
Land. Leaves painted the sidewalk with yellows and reds, the
remnants of two giant trees standing tall in front of the dark
grey stucco house. I stood on the front steps and looked at the
neighboring houses, wondered whether any of the inhabitants
would be like Paul, a new friend to bring me whiskey or let me
borrow eggs at midnight. I was excited about this new start—
new home, new city, new baby, new head space.

We took a walk around the neighborhood, ate at a French
eatery, stuffing our faces with decadent pastries, creamy pasta,
and a sweet little cannoli for dessert. We leisurely walked back
to the new house and made beds on the floor. It would be a

family slumber party in the center of the living room, since the moving truck was scheduled to arrive the next day.

But as night came, I reconsidered my moves. Did we make the right decision? Is this really a good place for our girls? Is the traffic going to turn me into a raging lunatic? Once we hit the edge of Los Angeles, it took two more hours to arrive at the address. We slept, we woke, we unpacked and hung old pictures on rented walls.

Over the next few weeks, we found new patterns for life in LA, but it was the first time we weren't helping in some capacity with church, which made the rhythm of life feel strange. It was the first time in my entire life, really. I missed our Denver community, the support and sense of belonging that sort of community gives. Singing with groups of people is a funny thing when you really think about it—all of us getting together and elongating words with different pitches, specific rhythms. But it had always connected me, grounded me, healed me. I felt like I was rudderless without that weekly rhythm, so I dragged Michael and the girls to church after church. But each time, I just got up and left in the middle, leaving Michael wide eyed and aghast that it had happened once again.

My body just had this reaction once I got there. I tried hard, but something in me didn't trust what was happening. It felt like suffocating with a hundred people around me smiling. I thought something was wrong with me, because everyone else looked so happy and fine. I remembered being those people and how good it felt. I didn't understand why I couldn't feel alive in that setting like I used to. I felt like a hurt animal—skittish and afraid of the tricks.

A wise woman named Hillary told me there are two parts to trauma. First, we feel the hit, like the impact of a crash. Then our bodies feel the effects long afterward. Maybe I didn't trust anyone because my body was still trying to protect itself. Every time I saw a man on a stage telling everyone else how to live their lives, I just couldn't shake the thought, *I don't believe you at all. You're telling us how to live, but you probably run yourself so ragged you never see your family. You're probably judging people and screwing someone behind your wife's back. You probably kicked gay people or your closest friend out of here because their ideas didn't line up with yours.* Harsh, yes. I hated my thoughts. But those thoughts transpired from years of those very experiences. *And oh, why is almost every preacher at these churches a white, able-bodied, straight, cisgender male? If my girls grow up here, will they be taught they are in second place? If my Lucie grows up here, where exactly will she be taught that she belongs? And while we're at it, do you guys really buy into this idea that God was first this bratty violent murderer who killed babies and desperately needed his son's blood in order to save all the rotten humans he accidentally created? Then suddenly had a change of heart and told everyone to love your enemies and turn the other cheek?*

I had some lengthly rants in my head. I didn't blame the speaker man. I knew he had his own circumstances that shaped him, just like I did. And I realized our celebrity culture doesn't stop at the entrance of the church. That kind of pressure is too much for anyone. I didn't judge the man. I just felt like we were all pretending he had the answer. I so wanted a place. I wanted the rhythm I had felt my whole life that revolved around church on Sunday. But inclusivity and equality were difficult to find. It made me wonder what I had built in my past, just what I'd contributed to that made some feel like they didn't belong. And it made me wonder why I would give myself to a religion that ultimately sees women in second place. It was puzzling to me how much I wanted to keep putting myself in that position, willing to overlook sexism to have a community to belong in. I guess it's up to each individual to decide what they can overlook, because no place will be perfect, but I knew I couldn't do that to myself anymore, and now it wasn't just me. I had these two little girls soaking it all in, their beautiful minds being formed right in front of my eyes. I couldn't program them to view themselves as second. So I wanted church, but I also didn't. I wanted the community without the inequality or blind buy-in. It frustrated me how I felt this new sight pulling me forward, yet I felt like I kept looking to the past. So I only felt weak, unable to move forward. The last year had been the hardest year of my life, hands down. I'd thought the pain of the last year would disappear with the simple swap of houses. I'd hoped that I'd jump over some sort of metaphorical line in the sand to everlasting bliss like Cinderella and her gang of mice. But that's not how life happens. Things don't change instantly, and it's not how our bodies heal from a crash or learn new patterns. So the new year came, and I was battling old versus new life patterns.

A typical day looked something like this:

6:00 a.m.: Baby wakes up, so I wake up. I'm the most positive mother ever in the whole universe. I'm gonna give this day a triple shot of happiness and kombucha.

7:30 a.m.: Fix a healthy breakfast for everyone. Lucie babbles and we cheer. Amelie dances around the house and we cheer. What a great family we are. I should post a pic on social media to let everyone know.

8:30 a.m.: Take Amelie to school. The insanity of Los Angeles traffic performs a double punch on my positive attitude.

9:30 a.m.: Physical therapy with Lucie. I'm told where she is on the chart compared with all the "normal" kids. I panic a little. I'm behind on teaching her so much, I better catch up.

11:30 a.m.: Healthy breakfast is countered with a donut for comfort.

1:00 p.m.: Pay bills, clean, avoid negative thoughts, try to write a song. *Why am I writing a song? Our career is in the gutter and a mean, powerful man is calling every single show we have and shutting it down. And why did our friend want us out of the church? And who exactly am I mad at? Myself. And everyone.*

3:00 p.m.: Pick up Amelie. Better eat a donut with her—no one likes to eat alone. More traffic. Collapse on the sofa and eat seaweed chips to counter the sugar. One girl runs wild, and the other makes booger bubbles in her nose while I say, "Say, 'Momma'! Lucie, you can do it! Say it like this, 'Mmmaaa-mmmaaa.'" I try to remember the tools the speech therapist gave me.

We go on a walk. A stranger on the street sees Lucie and says, "Oh, God bless you," or, "Oh, honey, she really is a light, really! She *really really* is! She is!" Which I know is supposed to be encouraging, but yeah, I *know* she is! Why do you keep repeating yourself? And I want to punch a stranger.

The beautiful world I saw this morning fills up with pollution and pain. The beautiful girl I saw this morning gets replaced with sadness because we have been working on everything longer than other kids have to and that feels so unfair. Everyone is trying to convince me that Lucie is an angel when I already know she is, but you know, she poops and vomits and screams like any ol' baby does. Amelie asks in tears, "Why does everyone talk to Lucie and tells you how cute she is but ignores me?" I breathe out a long sigh.

I try to explain and it feels unfair—to both of my girls. I'm trying so hard to be fair, divide my attention equally, care for everyone just the right amount, and I'm mad because I just really want someone to care for me the right amount and to go out on a date without barf on my boob.

6:00 p.m.: Dinner, wrestle the little one into pjs, comfort the older one's feelings about a new city and my own feelings of incompetence.

7:00 p.m.: Bedtime for kids. Wine time for me.

10:00 p.m.: Watch the news. "That's it, I guess we are f*#!@$."

6:30 a.m.: Repeat.

I was stuck on repeat, starting out positive, then crashing at the end of each day. I kept looking over my shoulder at what we had left behind in Denver and missing it with such a deep ache. I missed the community. I missed the feeling of home, and here I'd thought I was so great with change. I thought about Sacramento and how I'd seen the beauty of the world in a way that had begun to change me—the cow poop and the people and me were all in this beautiful rhythm of life. Then Lucie's birth had broken something wide open. I felt she was this answer to "Divine Mother, give me eyes to see." She was helping me see it all differently, but it felt like I was inside of a world I just didn't know yet, learning how to live all over again because the dot and the line had both thoroughly shaken me loose. The dot was no longer the true north, and the realization of that was disorienting, like waking up in a dark space and feeling my way through, not knowing up or down or forward or backward.

On one of those days that started out positive but slowly unraveled, I walked to our neighborhood bakery. They have the best pastries in town, and pastries give me love. I passed fig trees and houses, passed a lush garden that made me stop to examine a dozen flowers. The flowers didn't look too concerned about their place in the world. They didn't strive or have this incredible angst about their existence. I envied them. And I envied the mothers who looked so happy strolling their noncrying children along and laughing while finishing some phone conversation that was probably about their thriving business. *They must have been dealt a good hand*, I thought. *Me, I'm weak and stuck. We built a career and it crashed, and I'm pretty sure my identity crashed with it. Who am I now and how do I start over? I'm going to be that crotchety elderly woman who has twelve cats and her kids visit for only ten minutes at a time because she inevitably starts ranting about how life really gave her the middle finger. "You know, I used to sing once," I'll begin in a drunken stupor. But no one will be listening because twelve cats is a distraction and who really wants to hear such a pitiful ego story?*

I continued to the bakery. I walked to the stoplight and stopped short when I saw the writing spray-painted in stencil on the ground.

"These are the days," it said.

I stared at that dirty sidewalk and the words.

It made me recall a poem by Mary Oliver: "What will you do with your one wild and precious life?" My precious life. I stood there on the sidewalk, recalling the book and the poem. These are the days I get, that's it. And what am I going to do?

I knew I had seen a different side of life in the hospital. But my programed brain kept pulling me back to old habits, making me see through old lenses. My programed brain told me I needed to go back to the line, back to what I once knew. And my programed brain told me I needed to be afraid of what Lucie

would face and what I would face. It told me I needed to measure up, get our career back on track, be someone. I had seen this
other side of reality, but I kept falling into the same thought patterns out of habit and also a strange need for acceptance from
where I came from. So it was like I started waking up but kept
drifting back to sleep.

The words on the concrete asked it simply enough. Am I
going to keep going backward? Am I going to remain stuck? Just
what will I do with this time that I have?

I had a choice. It wasn't up to anyone else. Just me. I didn't
need to wait for a hero to rescue me or for my circumstances
to change. I had the power to change my thinking, to continue
opening my eyes. I had to choose it. I had to continue this journey that started before Lucie began and that broke wide open
with her birth. "Divine Mother, give me eyes to see."

I remembered a study by Charles Duhigg which claims that
40 percent of the things we do each day are habit and not actual
decisions. This made me think about my whole situation of seeing
the light and then lying in bed in tears, too weak to do anything.
I had a habit of seeing reality one way so I could see a new reality
in moments, but then my programed mind would let it slip away
as easily as water through fingers. It was like I was trying to hold
this new delicious water I had found in a bowl woven of straw. It's
like I kept trying to live on the line, but the line was gone.

This study about habits gave my brain and my body hope.
It helped me to know that I kept trying to go backward because
those habits were where I had lived for a really long time. The
line was the state of consciousness I used to live in. All of my
constructs had collapsed, but the habits remained deeply rooted.
I didn't want to keep seeing the old way, but my eyes and body

were trained to. I looked at those words scribbled on the sidewalk and decided I would not be a victim. I would not continue this pity party but instead would dig deeper into spiritual practices, deeper into centering mindfulness. I would keep retraining my brain and my body until it became second nature. I kept going with my prayer, "Divine Mother, give me eyes to see."

So like I had experienced for a moment in the dark water at the lake house, like I had touched on in Sacramento, I let my body unfurl, welcomed the weakness I saw in the world and in myself, not just speaking it, then hoping it passes, but welcoming it. I don't think I had done that before. I used to let myself feel it for a couple of days here and there but would cover it up quickly and try to be okay.

I stopped striving, stopped beating myself up for where I got it wrong. I let myself face it. I looked at what I had been running from, looked at the anger, the animal I had been suppressing and in effect causing to become an uglier thing. I took walks, wrestled, spoke out loud what I kept covering. I yelled out names I was angry with, people who had hurt me, names I had "covered in grace" thinking I had no right to be angry with them, and I realized I had really covered out of my own shame and fear. It was a continuation of opening my hands like in the car with Michael on the phone, like in Sacramento on the hilltop, like in the hospital with Lucie.

I lamented, a deep lament I hadn't let myself previously do. I let weakness teach me, instead of running from it. Like an addict speaking their frailty and addictions for the first time, I spoke mine.

I went all the way to the bottom of my fear—death. I was afraid one more thing would happen and it would do me in. I was afraid something would happen to Lucie, and I would lose her, then that would crush me, Amelie, and Michael, and it would mark us all in a way we couldn't ever heal from. So I faced that fear, dug into the heart of it in my morning meditations so it would lose its power. One morning when I was practicing this, I sat by a pond in the dark. The sun would be up in an hour. I held people I was angry at in my heart, felt love grow for them, felt my compassion grow for them. Then I held Michael in my heart, then Amelie, then Lucie. An image emerged in my mind: there were bushes across the pond, dark and tall. They grew and turned into a figure, a figure I understood to be death. Death looked at me and said, "I'm coming for you." And it shook me. I sat frozen on the dock of the pond, Death and me at a standstill, waiting for the other to make a move. But I remembered how I dove deep into the dark water in the lake, staring straight into the darkness and letting it wrap me up. I remembered death was not a bad thing in and of itself but a beautiful part of this life. I was tired of being taunted, waking each day in fear, ending each night wondering if the next day would crash or if something would happen and Lucie would not even wake up. I remembered the words on the sidewalk and recalled the light I felt at Lucie's birth. So I stood up, I looked at that shadowy figure across the pond with the most fierce and calm countenance I have ever felt, and I said, "Just come and get me."

The figure flew across the pond, and I didn't flinch or prepare to fight it. The strangest thing happened. It didn't give the violent blow I thought it would. It embraced me. And we sat on the dock as the slightest piece of the sun came up, Death and I.

It felt like I was making amends with my life, laying to rest all I was afraid of.

The Sight We Learn

You have your own stories, the dramatic
and more ordinary moments where what
has gone wrong becomes an opening to
more of yourself and part of your gift to
the world. This is the beginning of wisdom.

—KRISTA TIPPET

I made my way through the terminal to the baggage claim. We
had an acoustic show that night, and I remember being excited
to play and sing with people again. It had been a while since we
had a show. Songs were our therapy, and since we needed a lot of
therapy, we were writing almost all the time. We had a new song
called "Light." It emerged after the night Amelie and I splashed
around in the water at the lake, and I just wasn't sure I could
make it through the whole song because it was about Lucie and
I'm a crier.

I was going over the words to "Light" in my head as I
scanned the room for our baggage carousel number, and then
I saw them—a mother and her son, she smiling down at him,

and he beaming up at her. I noticed the features—small nose, almond-shaped eyes. He had Down syndrome. I had the urge to run toward them excitedly while waving Lucie in the air like some sort of country flag. "Look! Down syndrome! Awesome!" I wanted to scoop him up and squeeze his cheeks, give the mother a big hug, and chat up a storm like I had known her for years.

I didn't do any of this, for obvious reasons, such as scaring her child by suddenly scooping him up and because waving my baby in the air while yelling "Down syndrome!" felt like bad manners, as well as borderline appalling. But also because I did not have my Lucie with me. And, upon a second glance, I wasn't positive her baby had Down syndrome. I was pretty certain, but being pretty certain in cases like this is not something you want to gamble on. That would be a very Larry David moment, approaching a mother and congratulating her on her child with Down syndrome when he actually did not have it. I would think it was amazing, but I'm not quite sure what she would think. We parents are sensitive creatures.

The thing is that I was startled by the strength of these feelings, my feelings of connection and excitement. Yeah, our babies would be very different, but she would know what I knew. She would have the same secret thoughts, the same fears, experience the same thrill at hearing her baby swallow, know the angst of struggling and the elation of reaching each milestone. We would see each other in a different way, see each other's children in a different way. We had this little key that changed everything.

Suffering is what happens when we want what is in front of us to be different from what it is. Other people in the baggage claim area look at our little girl, and I can see it on their faces: they feel a mixture of things afterward, but first, they feel sorry.

I've done the same thing to other families. I was the one causing suffering. But that was before Lucie taught me. And now I have to restrain myself from scooping up strangers' children in public places and running with them down the street yelling, "Down syndrome!"

The patch of grass is mostly the same, though a little wilted because it is February in Denver. I'd walked this patch of grass on May 14, the day after Lucie was born. I am here again, almost three years later. It is right outside of the hospital, lined with bushes and flowers on one side, street on the other. I remember talking on the phone with two close friends, telling them about Lucie's heart conditions, staring at the grass and feeling like it all wasn't really happening. I stood there dazed and wondering whether I would have one daughter or two. How many people have stood here wondering the same thing, and how many got one—or none? This strip of grass feels like the divider between the regular world and the hospital world. On the left, houses, dogs, riding bikes, and on the right, sick babies, people waiting, wondering which side their baby will remain on.

This was where I began my state of consciousness about Lucie's life—a dot, a narrow definition that broke, expanded into a line, and now had broken into a different view.

I felt life split from before Lucie to after Lucie, from stuck in one consciousness to breaking into a new perspective. That day three years ago, I just stared at the grass, and I received a message from my cousin. Her son had had so many surgeries it was hard for me to keep them straight. Her text said, "Welcome to the heart club," and I didn't want to be part of the heart club.

I didn't want to know what it was like to be in her shoes or for Lucie to receive one more prick, test, or cut.

I wanted normal. I wanted safe. I wanted to face all of the regular scary things parents think about, not imagine a knife making a scar on Lucie's fragile skin. Lucie wasn't in the world long before it was making its mark on her. Heart club? No, thanks. I'd like to subscribe to something else—fruit, balloons, puppies.

I'd sat in this spot again when she'd had her second surgery at six months old, when our home was still empty and on the market and we lived at friends' houses, then the lake, then the road. I stood here after the social media blowup and our career took a solid downward plunge and Paul died. Three years ago Lucie was cut right down the center of her chest, and it felt like that is how all of life was—cut right down the center and laid open, uncertain how things would heal or what sort of scar would remain.

After we encounter tragedy, we often find ourselves asking, "If I could go back and give myself some advice, what would it be?" I think about what I would say to myself, maybe a word on how to deal with hateful people, a note that says, "You will be okay." Maybe I'd give a big speech about how this is one of the best things that will ever happen to me, so don't be so glum.

But I settle on this: I would walk up to that sad girl in the grass, give her a hug, and just keep walking. It's not that I didn't need the support, but I would get it. It's not that I didn't need to know I would be okay; I would be. I didn't need an answer or a ghostly figure to appear to help me believe it. I had to go through it all to believe it. I had to experience it.

New sight didn't come from someone giving me a summary on how to get through tough times. It came from hitting rock bottom, knowing what suffering is, feeling what love can do, and continuing to let both teach me in the years that followed.

I had to let people and experiences and my girls teach me moment by moment. My girls help me see. And if you want to know how Lucie continues to teach me to see, well, here it is:

She giggles.

She likes ice cream, but not pie.

She pretends to be a puppy at least once a day.

She likes it when I pretend to cry so she can kiss my head and say, "Oh, honey, it's okay!"

She likes her sister the most. I come in second.

She is supremely stubborn.

She is wildly happy.

She is the bossiest baby of all time, specifically to Amelie and me, not her daddy.

She is a risk taker, a little too much.

She smiles with her entire body.

She cries "nooooo!" and flails at every single nap time.

She tilts her head in the cutest way and softly says no in an attempt to avoid eating vegetables. She knows we think it's cute. She knows it makes us forget the vegetables.

She gives a good stink eye.

She loves Chance the Rapper and says, "Good God!" right on cue with him.

She likes to pinch people. Currently working on that.

She loves dance parties, can twerk, and screams when the music stops.

She has made adults stop and cry happy tears.

She hugs everyone. Because she sees the magic in everyone, not just in some.

I think understanding the utter magic of our bodies and our existence brings us into who we are meant to be. I'm learning this.

I walk this grass today and shake my head at how different I feel. I am not sad. I sometimes still worry about what Lucie might face. I hear what might come our way with her, and I hold my breath. But I'm not regretful, and I certainly am glad I didn't get "easy." Uncertain, obviously. Who isn't? What single person gets the stamp of certainty on their health or number of days? Not one. Though I am uncertain, I am not regretful. I am immensely grateful. The things I thought would crush me became the very things that made me see the world as more magical and vibrant than I ever have. This has all led to truer ground. It was not a blip in the road, a sad detour that could or should have been avoided. It was necessary. It was always the road we needed to be on, always walking toward this light I felt in the center of my being.

I'm more grateful for the moments I have because I'm paying more attention to the present, to what is right in front of me. I used to be constantly scared I would lose one of my daughters, or both of them. Constantly scared for their health and trying desperately to secure a shiny future for them. But my role is not to make this life easy for my girls but to give them a springboard, to help keep their child hearts alive and open, to guide them with love so they can navigate their own circumstances and choices. I see more clearly what Lucie and Amelie are—not something that can be taken away or snuffed out.

"Oh death, where is your sting?"

I understand a bit now because death is part of life. It was never separate from it. Death is not evil in and of itself, and so death cannot take away what Lucie is or will be on the other side of life. I worry less, do more celebrating, more dancing, more star gazing, more magical living.

I still have the hard days of sleep deprivation, crying at 4:00 a.m., diapers, sibling fights that leave everyone a wreck, barf on my pants and shirt—the oh-so-classy world of parenting. I still see harsh comments online or receive them right to my face, comments on how we have fallen into the deep end, how we throw the word love around to too many people. And to that I'd say, "Oh, thank you, I'm trying to."

I wouldn't trade our story for anything, not ever.

Because seeing this side of life isn't something that comes easily. This perspective change was slow and gradual, and now that I've seen it, I can't unsee it. This is the sight we learn only by living, only through practice.

I stood here on this patch of grass as Lucie got a cut right in the center of her chest. It healed fast, leaving a scar composing one solid line with one single dot at the bottom where the chest tube and some wires used to be. One day while she danced naked with her sister and friends, a little girl friend said, "Oh, look! Lucie has an exclamation point on her chest!" All of the kids cheered for it and wished they had one too.

I wonder how she will view this scar when she is older. I hope with pride, because this scar is beautiful. Her scar is a mark that we and everyone who knows her celebrate. For me, it's a reminder of what we all went through, what she went through, of the doctors I hold in unbelievable respect, the gift they gave us. I hope she sees this scar and is not ashamed but knows her body is a work of art, perfect from moment one.

I also love this scar because it is fitting. Yes, she has lived up to the meaning of her name thus far, but that word "light" alone sounds a little too soft. She is wilder and brighter like a strobe or a floodlight. So an exclamation point seems to go right with her name. It's "Lucie!"

I am thankful our career crashed.

I am thankful faith crashed.

I am thankful for surgery.

I am thankful for Paul's life and death.

I am thankful for everything and everyone—most of the time.

One night in the basement of a church in Denver, we gathered in a circle again. Lights danced on faces. The place was packed. I never imagined we would stand here again. Never imagined we would be invited back to this church after such a tumultuous experience for everyone. There were many familiar faces, many new. Some that were there on the very first night we started this church. I hugged them and was a mess for the remainder of the evening as we sang and talked and laughed together. We talked about doubt and how it pushes us toward truth. We talked about the wonder of this divine mystery we all kept gathering around.

At one point I looked over to Michael. It's amazing to me how far we've come. We not only like each other but love each other more now than at our start. We see each other's true selves more now than sixteen years ago, still laugh at each other's jokes, still think the other has interesting and profound things to say. We have more dance parties than ever, still laugh way too hard when the other farts, and still steal each other's phone chargers and then fight about it. I'm lucky to have someone around who steals anything of mine, because that means we are still doing life together.

When a couple has children, it's obviously beautiful, but the sorting out of tasks and sleep deprivation gets hard. And then when a creative, unorganized, noncommittal couple has a kid, lose their faith, then have a kid who needs heart surgery, and then they move . . . Well, you know the story. We had lived in love and a whole lot of war.

There was a time I really wasn't sure where we would end up. We both felt close to insanity many times over, accused the other of jumping over the edge many times over. But we both experienced moment upon moment of our hearts opening, experiencing love, seeing each other. We chose forgiveness, over and over again. We chose love, over and over again. And to love is the most profound thing I know. Love is the narrow road, not the wide one. I mean, have you ever tried to truly love unattached? It isn't what the masses are going for. It will leave you dropping all of your belongings and baggage as you go because there just isn't room for all of that.

So I looked at him and knew full well just how amazing it is that we love each other, especially after all of this, especially so fully.

We played our show that night, told our story, sang Christmas songs and other songs. People sang so loudly it was difficult to pick individual voices out of the crowd. There were no performers or observers; we had become one voice.

After the songs, we stayed long into the night talking with new and old friends, and the thing I kept hearing was, "I used to believe this, and now I see it differently."

At first we felt completely alone, felt our career, faith, and life crumble, but now it was like something had been unlatched. We received letters from people expressing solidarity. "I have had questions my entire life, and now I finally feel the freedom to ask them, to let go, to open my heart again." "I have felt alone for years, was about to end it all, and now I know I'm not alone." "My child has special needs. We have found so much joy connecting with your story." It was shocking. We kept being honest about our journey even when it was painfully hard, and others began letting us know about their own journeys.

We were all experiencing this perspective shift. Something gave us eyes to see what we couldn't on our own.

Never did I imagine this happening, feeling this kind of inclusivity. There was something profoundly healing in coming back to this basement where so much was born and so much had died. It felt like coming home after two years of being in rehab. I thought the story would be different, the lessons learned faster and easier while everyone was still in the same place. But we really don't know just what will happen when we ask, "Open my eyes." It may hurt more than we think if we are thoroughly grounded in a perspective. But the journey is a vital one. Our political, social, and very ecological climate hangs in the balance. What we value, how we take care of what we value, how we view each other—it affects everything. Our perspective of the world informs what we put our hands to do or destroy. "Open my eyes" isn't just a nice sounding refrain; I believe it is vital to the future of humanity. Who and what we are opening our eyes to affects who and what we are opening our future to. If we keep our eyes shut, much will be lost around us and within us. We will not only miss but kill this very beautiful life and world. I used to believe there was some line between what is sacred and common, miraculous and mundane. My perspective had to shift to see that actually all of the bushes are burning, the entire world is ablaze.

The Most Beautiful Thing I've Seen

But I'll tell you what hermits realize. If you go off into a far, far forest and get very quiet, you'll come to understand that you're connected with everything.

—ALAN WATTS

I was looking at fog lying on the hills of Ojai, watching it rest and breathe. It swelled, then fell over the hill and hovered. There is something about being in nature that reminds me that I was born out of this ground, connecting me to the things I am made of. I was using this day to keep following the prayer I prayed every morning and evening: "Divine Mother, give me eyes to see."

I thought about the dot and the line, and now this new, wide-open space. The dot I came from was always my true north. It's what was ingrained in me from the start, and so I'd continued to look over my shoulder at it, walking on the line and looking back to see just how far I could stretch it. I ran as far as I could from fundamentalism, from structures and divisions that harm, stretched the line out as far as I could until it shook and couldn't be stretched anymore. It was still tied to my true north—the dot. And so it did what any thing that is stretched to the max eventually does. It broke.

What I used to see—a single way to live, and these bodies of ours as broken from the start. I saw a world to escape. And what I see now—the ground of being beneath and around it all, not confined to religions or tribes, a good world good from the start and still becoming, beating and spinning out.

I have been on a mission to see and feel the world with new eyes and a new heart. I have been on a mission for friends and strangers to see Lucie, truly see who she is in all her essence. Her birth flipped our lives around, and I needed to let you know about the beauty that is her and the beauty that is you. Maybe if I could explain it all, just what I see now, maybe you could believe you are good as well, see it all with new eyes, have the courage to live the way you know deep down you were made to live.

As a lot of journeys go, we find an X in the ground, demanding us to dig more. This is what happened to me as I lay on the ground that day in Ojai, thinking about all of this change. I began to pray, then meditate, and I experienced a profound sort of vision or dream.

A pointed, unnerving question came into my mind. *You see Michael, you see your girls, you see me, the Divine Mother, with new eyes, but how do you see yourself?*

I wasn't sure what I thought. I imagined someone else

looking at me and wondered what their thoughts would be. Again, the question came back into me.

No, no, not someone else's view, yours. How do you see yourself?

I paused. I didn't really want that question. I wanted that question turned toward others, toward the world, because all of that was looking quite beautiful. It made me think about the moments I had faced my weakness, let the darkness wrap me up and heal me. Just what did I see in myself after facing all of that?

I didn't want that question because honestly, when I faced myself, I saw something incomplete. I saw someone trying really, really hard to belong in this world. I'm trying to convince people that my Lucie belongs in this world and that they belong in this world, but that message is coming from a heart that doesn't know its own worth.

I like to think I am fighting this fight for Lucie, for my girls, but it isn't just about them. It's about me too, this deep need to know my life means something. I believe Lucie is perfect, but really, I don't even believe that about myself.

Then, in my imagination, I saw myself as a child. I was surrounded by dark purple and blue, but I saw something in my hands, a light. I just looked at this little girl and my heart unfolded. I saw something kind. Something vulnerable, diligent, and honest. I saw myself as both sweet and strong. It suddenly seemed so wrong to see what was lacking when looking at this child, because she really wasn't lacking anything. She was fully herself and good.

I looked at her and thought, *I like this girl*. And it suddenly clicked how my view of self shapes my entire life. It shapes my daughters' lives. It shapes everyone I come into contact with. How I value myself gives others permission to use the same measure of value. I try hard to make others see my daughter's essence, but how can I when I don't know my own?

Then a chain of images unfolded and the dream continued.

I saw Amelie, or rather I saw from behind Amelie's eyes. Amelie the strong, wild, loving girl. In the dream, I was her, and I saw myself from her eyes, saw Lucie from her eyes, saw her daddy from her eyes. She was making sense of life, carefully considering our actions and reactions. Considering Lucie, how her sister is different, but the same. How she struggles with her own purpose, wondering why we are here and whether her own body is good. Then she wrapped Lucie up and ran, an intense sister bond. They laughed, played, interacted with the world in a way I don't. I saw that Amelie has her own perspective on it all, her own dot she is starting from.

Then the scene changed again and I was looking from behind a smaller child's eyes, this time Lucie's. She ran from the side of the sofa to the kitchen table. She was laughing, full of life, full of excitement, wondering what was around each corner. She was present, looking for me but not needing me to fill a need, just looking to see my face.

There was so much joy and love within her, so much thrill, looking for the next thing to destroy, the next thing to empty out, not out of anything but wonder. There was only wonder. Life through the eyes of a child—it was more vivid than I had imagined, more alive and enchanting. *Whoa, this is wild,* I thought. *Seeing life through the eyes of my daughters, their perspective. This is what I need—to see the world through my daughters' eyes. They are just existing in this beautiful moment, not needing to write it down or make sense of it, just experiencing.*

But it didn't stop. The scene changed quickly, and I was looking at something else.

I was looking at my mother.

She was sitting in a garden looking right back at me. I had seen this picture before, a grainy Polaroid from years ago when she was around fifteen or sixteen years old.

My mother, whom I have not seen eye to eye with for so long. We had taken steps toward each other, but our views on just about everything had shifted so drastically—from politics to religion to how to raise our children in this new secularized Western society with social media and AI. Our ideas on who is in and who is out are different. Our views on Down syndrome are different. Our views on what we are doing on this earth is different. So I was looking at her and seeing something different from myself, something to fight against, something to change.

But the scene changed again and I saw my mother as a child. She was timid with a beautiful heart, peeking around the corner of her kitchen wall, looking at me, conveying in a moment all of the things I never understood. She was showing me her perspective, what she saw, how her childhood was. *This is the world I saw. This is my frame of reference. This is the spot I hid in when I was afraid. This is the garden and yard I adventured in when I was happy. This is how I saw it.*

Then I saw her as an adult. I saw her sitting and considering something, a decision she had to make, and it made my heart break. She was physically alone and also felt emotionally alone, so she decided alone, and her life continued.

Then the scene changed again. I saw the world from her eyes. I saw all the ways she had sacrificed and given. I saw her look at her babies—my brother and sister—saw her look at me. She held and loved me, thought I was perfect at my very start.

I looked through her eyes and saw myself grow. We were connected. Walking the same terra-cotta tile to the kitchen, looking out the same windows. Then at some point, we were arguing in a car. It was a bad fight, possibly our worst as we drove along the beautiful coastline in California, just trying so hard to merge two different perspectives. I saw myself looking straight at her with frustration, and she at me with the same. We couldn't understand each other and just couldn't get past this wall of difference.

I so want the world to understand my child, but I don't understand my own mother. She wants the world to understand her, but she doesn't understand her own daughter—why she left the faith and the tribe she raised her in. She tried so hard, loved so much. And then I was back in my own self, looking again at my mother in the garden with her swimsuit and lean legs. It felt like I was seeing her for the first time. I was looking at her, her at me, and I saw myself.

How do you see yourself?

I saw myself as her.

This beautiful creature kneeling in the garden, I was her and I was wrestling my own heart.

I saw a golden line slowly thread through her and me. It ran through us, then to my girls, to Michael, and back around in a circle—it connected all of us. Then the golden circle of thread spun out like a net to everyone else.

I didn't just understand that we are all a part of each other; I felt it. It is one thing to understand you have a right arm, but to feel air prickling the skin of that arm is an entirely different thing. It's one thing to be taught the concept of love, another to experience it in your entire body. This was that—I was experiencing our connection, seeing we were connected and existing in a circle.

The most beautiful thing I have seen were the eyes of my mother gazing out at me from that garden, and in her eyes I saw myself, my girls, my husband, the intrinsic and esoteric connection of everything and everyone.

I think I felt this when I was knit and spun, then I grew and forgot for a multitude of reasons. I felt shame, felt broken, then had a child the world called broken, yet I began to see she was good from her start. I couldn't see my own goodness, my own magical body, or my mother's goodness, her own sacred life. I think we know our connection at our first moments. We just need the eyes to see it again.

Moment One

**Stop acting so small. You are the
universe in ecstatic motion.**

—Rumi

First moments, the merging of two cells into one, multiplying—
two, four, six, eight—rapidly growing and forming the information
that will decide my hair, eyes, teeth, hands. My DNA—everything
I need to become a human—and still I am invisible to the naked
eye. I am grown from my mother's own body, blood from her blood,
heartbeat from hers, making her belly swell and hormones go crazy
with rage and the desire for cream-filled donuts at 4:00 a.m.

My body grows and she puts a hand upon her belly to feel a
foot kick her side, the jerk of hiccups, the roundness of my head.
She is proud, proud of her body that is a force, a source of life
to mine.

I grow. Her body tells her it is time. I come into the world
with pain and euphoria as she breaks her beautiful body to give
me life. She sees me for the first time, what she has made, and
it is good. The intricacy of the human body is staggering—veins,

heart, lungs, synapses, toenails, chemicals, eyelashes, all good and beautiful. She holds my body and breathes in.

I grow. From a baby to a toddler, from a toddler to a little girl. I am four and I can run around with my shirt off and feel the fullness of the wind. I can paint my belly and take baths with my friends, slap my butt and laugh. We sleep under stars and run through sprinklers naked and wild. We are silly and think our bodies are strange and wonderful, we think the world is full of magic.

I grow and I am six. I am taught what tribe I am in and what traditions we keep. I am taught what I can and cannot do with my body. I can no longer take my shirt off outside on my front porch, no longer run around outside naked with my friends with paint on our bellies because the man across the street stares, so my mother takes me inside and tells me I am now the age where I need to be careful.

A feeling comes I've never known before. I learn later the word for it is shame.

I am at a friend's house and a teenage boy keeps making me sit on his lap. I don't understand it. We are all sitting in a circle, about ten of us, and no one notices. I am confused and try to get away from him, but he holds me there and moves his hands in a way I don't understand. I feel I should obey because he is a strong older boy and I am a small girl inherently weaker than he. I get mad that my body is not stronger, that I cannot break free. I feel it is my fault. Maybe I should not have worn shorts so my legs would be covered.

And then there is the church leader, my friend's father, who insists I stay in the bathroom with him. I don't want to, but I feel I have to obey because he is a man and I am young and born the lesser of the sexes. It is uncomfortable and I think he must not know what he is doing. A respectable man, let alone a church leader, wouldn't do this. I stay, then I run. And now I am older and know better. Yes, he knew.

So I am six and I can no longer be free in this body or world I once ran wild in, but I should cover my body because there are predators. The beautiful connected world gets divided; I become divided.

I am fourteen. I feel my body changing on me. I notice and others notice, and I no longer have the freedom of my youth. Blood comes, and I am embarrassed, hiding my runs to the grocery store, keeping it a secret, wondering whether my brother laughs when he looks under the sink. It is a wonder, growing into womanhood, but I am starting to hate being a woman. I am ashamed of what my body does. This beautiful thing that I once ran free in is turning on me, making me awkward and uncomfortable.

Some eyes consume rather than see. I am told this is my fault. I am told God wants me to cover my body, wear longer skirts and shirts up to my collarbone and to be sure they aren't tight. But how much skin is okay? Because other girls cover their whole bodies in black, and I hear of the time when there were two separate staircases for males and females so that males wouldn't accidentally catch a glimpse of an ankle.

Now that I am fourteen, now that I am changing, is God ashamed with what he made, this body and this vibrant planet? The body formed in my mother, so good and beautiful, has it turned to shame with age and religious threads? If this body is not holy in and of itself, then God never should have made it in the first place. It's the flower hating its vibrant petals, the beautiful tree sprouting from the earth only to grow and be ashamed of its bark.

I am twenty. I have rejected the shy, awkward aspects of womanhood and instead learned to joke about it to cope and be cool. But when night comes, I am often afraid to walk down the street alone. Every walk I take is accompanied by fear, because I see the eyes consume. I hear the threats and am followed. I have friends who are victims. Every girl I know has been afraid, every one of them.

One hid in the laundry basket when she was nine. One silently prayed every night from thirteen to sixteen that her father would be too drunk to come into her bed. One hid from her brother, another from her grandfather, another from her husband. Some say it is the woman's fault the shirt was too low, her breasts too big. How can anyone resist? But here's a staggering thought: maybe the victim isn't at fault. If in looking at the beautiful body you cannot appreciate beauty but must strip and consume, then it is true our culture has poisoned our minds—consume, take, be the animal, take, take, take.

Shame. Did my mother think of shame when she held me close to her chest at my birth? Was she ashamed? The beautiful form shifts as if through a dark kaleidoscope: good, beautiful, pure, broken, shamed, used. All held together by a story of a serpent and a girl. Though some claim the curse is broken, some still believe it—the body is shamed, the curse ever present; the world we were meant to thrive in is something to escape.

I am thirty. I have made two girls within my own body, felt the rush of bringing them into the world, and when I saw their bodies, I saw a miracle. Their skin and eyelashes perfect. Tiny lips, tiny fingernails, eyes embodying innocence and awe.

They grow and run around my house naked and scream wildly without self-awareness or social concern. They paint their bellies with a smiley face, a flower. "There is magic in the soil, Momma! Come look!" Fireflies are fairies and stardust is what they hold in their hands—a magical world.

I teach them about our culture and what is and isn't acceptable. But what I will not teach them is to be ashamed of their bodies.

They were beautiful from moment one, and that will not change—not with age, not with anything. One daughter looks at her body in the mirror. We talk about the organs and skin, how her body will change. She is beautiful on every count. I remember when I was six, and I know I have to warn her. Not shame her, but tell her how some people were not taught to love but take for themselves, and she must be brave and aware. It pains me as I tell her, her innocent mind not knowing why one person would hurt another in such a way.

"Do not be afraid," I tell her. "But this is our culture, so be smart and be aware, my brave girl."

Shame teaches us, but I will not teach my daughters in this way. I will try to empower them to be proud of their bodies, respectful of their bodies, in awe of how miraculous they are and what they are capable of.

I will tell my daughters that to be a woman is not to be lesser, not to be an object, not to be owned. She is not a body to exploit or a product to be consumed.

"She" is not shame.

"She" is beautiful woman with beautiful body, capable of cosmic realities. Holding someone close, experiencing love, making love, creating life, accepting another human life as her own, feeling pain, joy, giving strength, healing with a kiss, bringing wholeness with a touch, giving nourishment with her own body.

"She" is wise enough to follow, grounded enough to lead, if it's leading a child or leading a nation. The woman's body is made in the image of Love, from Love herself, Life herself, so she herself is of God.

See it, beautiful woman, you are good. See it, beautiful man, intersex, human, you are intrinsically good, perfectly good.

Perfect from moment one.

EPILOGUE

And now, Mother,

Here we are. I've explained the whole thing. I didn't realize what emotions I would unearth or lay to rest.

You grew me and taught me. I loved you, then fought you, then discovered just who you are, and in the process I discovered who I am. I hope this has helped you understand the path I have been on. I know it has helped me understand it.

We will surely still wrestle each other when we don't think the other is fair. We may scream at each other when it hurts too much to open our eyes. But I will also turn my face toward your light, knowing that each breath is a gift given by you.

What do I see now? I see you. I see you more clearly than I have before.

I promise to tell you more about what I am experiencing and feeling. To tell you about the little and big things so that this connection remains open.

Here's something: we just bought a trampoline. Yesterday the girls and I were jumping on it, and it reminded me of the back yard in our tiny hometown. Our feet hit the black stretched mat, sending drops of liquid light dancing around our legs. We laid out flat so that water pooled, then filtered from the top to underneath, gathered and then dropped.

I was tense and scared yesterday—of fires, of news from across the world, of foreign powers, of overdue earthquakes. I lay on the black mat while Amelie jumped wild, Michael sprayed her with water, and Lucie yelled and laughed and backed away to the farthest edge.

I lay there and looked up into the sky as everything moved around me. Wondering what lies beyond this dot I am so carefully organizing for my girls, this control I believe I have, but don't. This is the springboard I am creating for them, and I wonder what my girls will say about it. Too open? Too safe? Amazing and the best life ever? Or will they say their parents are super weirdos and don't have a solid grasp on reality or on how to see things right?

Maybe. My girls and I see most things the same right now, but it won't always be that way. I wonder what they will deconstruct, construct, what they will run from or keep.

Right now is the moment I have, to see and feel it fully. I lie on my back. The sky is clear, matching my eyes, a color I see as blue.

AFTERWORD

This story is not a roadmap for everyone else. I'd love to have the answers—oh, that would do a lot for my ego. But just like I had to listen, you need to listen. Your teachers may not tell you the same things mine told me, and they will not be silent if you are patient and willing to find them in the most unlikely places.

It is not just the wise man who hands us his wisdom but the person who rubs us like gritty sandpaper and makes us scream. If you keep finding the sandpaper person, let them teach you. There is most likely something you don't like about them that has more to do with you than with them. You will find your teachers on front porches, or you'll find teachers that come out of your very body. And creation—I am finding the more I am silent and listen to the soil and trees, the more I let the wind catch me up, the more alive I am.

I have begun to recognize everything and everyone as my teachers. My classrooms were the dot and everyone within it, the line and everyone within it, and now the circle and all of you within it. I am grateful for it all. It was leading from one thing to the next, always teaching, always whispering, "Look this way. Open your eyes."

I'm still listening. I wake early in the morning and listen

before the world wakes up and tells me who I am. When my eyes cloud over and I forget, I listen and let the Divine Mother tell me, remind me again.

What I see now:

Myself: Like a great pine tracing its own rings in awe, I was given eyes to see myself. Like a person with amnesia, I remembered my name and what I am in relation to all of this beauty, pain, and light.

I now see myself as both strong and weak, and the combination doesn't scare me. I see myself as still learning but complete, still becoming and already belonging. I am not ashamed of my story. When I am tempted to pick shame back up, I see that child self and remember to love her. I like how my voice sounds and how my body looks. I like my jokes and my wrinkly hands. This is not big ego. This is a woman who is no longer insecure, which on this side of things is really something.

It seems this whole journey of sight leads us right into the center of ourselves at some point. We look outward and hope to God we see a world that is good and worth it. Then the sight inevitably turns inward and we hope to God we are good and worth it.

The wounds I've written about in this book opened up all of the places I was scared to look. And in that forced cold stare, I first saw deathly creatures ready to trap and swallow. A monster waiting to devour with a thousand tiny bites, like ants on a worm. But that darkness was an invitation into the depth of an undiscovered ocean bed. And there was no monster lurking in the deep. Just a creature like myself wanting to be loved.

So I wrapped that creature up, looked at her from all sides and angles until she lost her darkness. She was the most beautiful teacher, direct, good. She slowly unfurled into vibrant fractals of light as I stared openmouthed and with this great understanding—this world is sneakier than I thought; more mysterious and filled with wonder than I had boiled things down to. And I am all that beautiful light.

My family: My girls are more mysterious to me than ever. I see them as wild and funny, intuitive, and the face and voice of the Divine Mother. We still fight. We all still lose it at times, like today when one was sick and the other emotional and I a combination of both. I am still learning how to parent; they are still learning how to be parented. I'm also still learning how to be a student, letting them teach. I do more learning than they do.

Both of my girls are art pieces of their own. To think that at first I thought there was some measuring stick for these magical things. These bodies are more wondrous than I thought—all of the healing and tricks they can do like love or feel or grow. Sometimes I stare in wide-eyed awe at them, and sometimes I still lock myself in the bathroom to get a little peace and quiet from all of that emotional wonder.

I see Michael more clearly than I ever have and now can see what love is. In oneness—I see us as exactly that. That doesn't mean a static perfection or the absence of absurd fights, but I see his essence and I honestly don't think I did before. I'm learning to love him unattached and fully. It's better than owning or loving in moderation. He is the heart of me and I of him.

Everything else: We can spend a good portion of our lives wondering whether we belong here. It seems someone airdropped us into this violent paradise without a roadmap and expected us to know what to do. But we were born of this earth that eats itself to grow, evolved out of its ground and started looking around just like everything else. The divine gave birth to all of this divine.

Now I see so much spinning and singing I can hardly take it all in. I saw spider webs blowing in the breeze today, and it seemed like the greatest artist swooped in and left all of this glistening light dripping off of branches. The once spider-predator was now a glorious artist. I still feel the anguish of violence, lament this ongoing war dance, just with more awareness and practice to keep my heart open so I don't miss the very present beauty. I'm more open to weep with those who weep and dance with anyone who is having a dance party, like the holy rollers or our wild meditation friends in Los Angeles. Or Lucie—she is always having a dance party.

The way we see something changes how we treat it. If I believe I am staring at the enemy, my violent programing will likely raise my fists. If I believe I'm staring at a person who needs to be fixed, my agenda will inevitably blind me.

Maybe that's what Jesus did when the soldiers came for him. Maybe he didn't force himself to give his body to the enemy. Maybe he didn't see the enemy at all. Maybe he saw himself, or you, or me.

If I truly believe this body and world are something to escape, I will only suffer. But if I believe I am looking at the face of God, I will stare in awe every time. It's all in how you see it.

ACKNOWLEDGMENTS

I have so much gratitude for this team of people:

My agent, Angela Scheff: You are a genuinely amazing human! Thank you and Chris Ferebee for taking this book on and giving so much support and guidance.

Stephanie Smith: I read your letter asking me to write a book an entire year after you sent it. Thank you for not giving up easily. And thank you for helping me believe I could actually do this, for hearing me out as I stumbled through my story, through all of the arranging and rearranging. You were always encouraging, always helping me find the deepest heart of it.

Thanks to David Morris, my publisher: I'm so grateful you were willing to take this book on. It was a pleasure talking through this story with you and Stephanie in that ever-so-fancy Chili's after our show. Thank you for believing in this.

Thanks to my marketing director, Alicia Kasen: I'm so thankful for all of your hard work and for hearing me out when I changed my mind time upon time. To Jennifer VerHage, PR manager: Thank you for helping me get this book into people's hands, for doing the part I am terribly bad at! Curt Diepenhorst, thank you so much for your cover designs and for giving it your best. I'm so grateful for your beautiful artistry. You were inspiring and a pleasure to work with. Thank you! Thank you to my copyeditor, Brian Phipps: Your dedication to get it just right amazed me. You made this book better.

For the entire team: I know there is so much work that went into publishing this book, and I couldn't have done it without you. I'm deeply grateful for such an amazing team. Thank you all!

Everyone has been a teacher, everyone inspiring or pushing me to dig in deep. I am grateful for everyone I have run into on my path, and all of you who have read this story, thank you.

For our fan friends: Thank you for supporting our art through the years, for letting us change and be honest. Thank you for driving to house shows or arenas and for your continued love.

Bloom family: You made life rich. Thank you for your love. It changed us and you will always feel like home. To the Liturgists: Thank you for being vulnerable and creating a place for people to belong.

To my friends: Some of you slept on a hospital floor more than once for us, stayed close in my toughest times. We've cheered each other on through jobs, births, deaths, triumphs, weddings, rehab, surgery, and so much more. We traversed a lot of good life together and I love you all.

For my family: Thank you for the pine-cone wars and playing chase in the dark, for the holiday traditions and love that have gotten us through some tough times. Anna for giving me so much strength, and Cody for giving me so much heart. Mom and Dad for giving me everything you could and are still giving now. For my stepmother: Thank you for joining this crazy family and loving our girls so well. For my second family, the Gungor side: I got lucky with all of you. I met you all at just seventeen years old, and nineteen years later you feel as much like family as my own. Thank you for your immense love and support, weirdo dance moves, late-night debates, and incredible commitment to family. I love you all.

For my girls: What mother got so lucky as me? You have taught me not to look to the past or future but to be here now. You have reminded me to look someone right in the eyes instead of awkwardly glancing. You remind me to listen, to stay curious, silly, loud, wild. You have unearthed the wonder of what it means to be a woman and a mother. Amelie: You are an old soul. An amazing combination of wild and thoughtful, strong and considerate. A budding philosopher and adventurer. You have this love in you that calms and sees what a lot of us can't. And Lucie: You were strong from the start. You came into this world in a blaze and you haven't stopped lighting everything up. You make me look at the dirt and the flowers and make me dance when I don't want to. You are insanely funny and have made me laugh right in the middle of crying; you help me fully experience life. You already make this world better. You both are two of the greatest teachers I will have.

For my love: I have been stuck on just what to say here. How do you thank someone who feels like your very self? It's like thanking your own arms for staying attached to your body or your own heart for beating, and "thank you" is just too short. But still, thank you for choosing to lean in and see me when I'm crazy-eyed and scary or when I can't remember who I am. Your risk and heart have broken through immeasurable amounts of tough ground. I love your heart for truth, and I love your chubby toes, kind eyes, strong love. I'm beyond grateful that you are part of my spiritual path and I yours, beyond grateful that you yelled across that parking lot and asked me to have pancakes more than eighteen years ago. I'm grateful for how I have known you: Michael, the boy I met, and Vishnu Dass, the soul who was discovered. Let's grow older and weirder together.